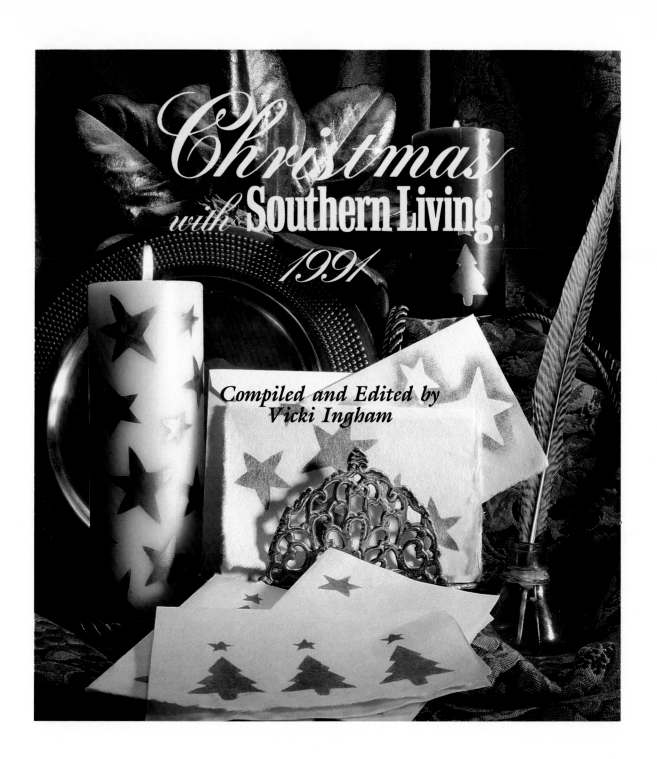

Christmas with Southern Living 1991

Compiled and Edited by
Vicki Ingham

Oxmoor House®

©1991 by Oxmoor House, Inc.
Book Division of Southern Progress Corporation
P.O. Box 2463, Birmingham, Alabama 35201

Southern Living® is a federally registered trademark belonging to Southern Living, Inc.

Library of Congress Catalog Card Number: 84-63032
ISBN: 0-8487-1025-8
ISSN: 0747-7791
Manufactured in the United States of America
First Printing

Executive Editor: Nancy Janice Fitzpatrick
Director of Manufacturing: Jerry Higdon
Art Director: Bob Nance
Copy Chief: Mary Jean Haddin

Christmas with Southern Living 1991

Editor: Vicki L. Ingham
Assistant Editor: Heidi Tyline King
Contributing Editors: Margaret Allen Northen,
    Kathleen English
Recipe Editors: Susan Payne, Foods Editor, and Kaye Adams,
    Test Kitchens Director, *Southern Living*® magazine
Editorial Assistants: Catherine S. Corbett, Karen Brechin
Assistant Copy Editor: Susan Smith Cheatham
Production Manager: Rick Litton
Associate Production Manager: Theresa L. Beste
Production Assistant: Pam Bullock
Artists: Barbara Ball, David Morrison
Designer: Carol Middleton

To find out how you can order *Southern Living* magazine, write to *Southern Living*®, P.O. Box C-119, Birmingham, AL 35283

Contents

Introduction

Dressing up the house for Christmas can do more than anything else to put you in a holiday mood. When you trim the tree, line the mantel with candles and greenery, and hang a fat wreath on the door, you create a festive atmosphere that sets the stage for celebration.

Last year when we set out on our Christmas travels to gather stories for this year's book, we found great decorating ideas almost everywhere we looked. That's why in this edition you'll find inspiration and how-to's not just in "Decorating for the Holidays," but in "Christmas Around the South" and "Holiday Traditions," too. Many of the projects in "Christmas Bazaar" are also decorations, ones you'll want to make for your own home as well as for gifts.

Once you've decorated your house, it's only natural to want friends and neighbors to come enjoy it with you. To make your entertaining easy and pleasurable, "Celebrations from the Kitchen" offers dozens of mouth-watering recipes that you can mix and match for parties, luncheons, and formal dinners.

This is a companionable season, one that focuses on the blessings of family and friendship and inspires generosity and compassion. Whether your festivities are large or small, your gift list long or short, may all that you do this season be infused with the joy and love that are the hallmarks of Christmas.

Christmas
Around the South

Above: Nineteenth-century paintings of sporting scenes hang on the walls of the drawing room, which looks as it did when Harvey Ladew lived here. For the Christmas open house, board president Martha Robbins decorated the mantel with magnolia, ivy, boxwood, nandina, andromeda, and Harry Lauder's walking stick (Corylus avellana contorta). *Gold spray paint adds highlights to the natural materials.*

Harvey Ladew's Legacy

"I cannot imagine going through life without a great many hobbies," wrote Harvey S. Ladew. "Friends have tried to convince me that I should 'stick to one thing' and they usually pull the old bromide about 'Jack of all trades.' I personally think that Jack is the guy who is having the most fun out of life."

Harvey Ladew, born in New York City in 1887, spent his life having a great deal of fun. He loved horses and fox hunting, as well as painting, sculpture, gardening, and music. He traveled widely—not only to the usual places in Europe, but also to Moscow via the Trans-Siberian railway and across the Arabian desert to Persia via camel caravan. One adventure in 1913 even made the headlines of the *New York Herald*: Ladew and some of his family were sailing around the world on his uncle's yacht when the Japanese seized the vessel and arrested the entire party. His memoirs do not explain how they extricated themselves from this situation.

Although Ladew had little interest in his father's leather-belting business, he felt duty-bound to oversee it after his father's death. Then when America entered World War I, he joined the army and served as a liaison officer in France. After the war, the business was sold, and the profits assured Ladew of a comfortable income. He therefore decided "to reverse the plan followed by most American men: I would enjoy my youth and health while they lasted, hunt in England during the winter and spend the rest of the time visiting all the far-off places I longed to see; then, when I was half a century

Above right: A topiary hunter and hounds race across the lawn at Ladew Topiary Gardens in Monkton, Maryland. Red bows dress the figures for Christmas.

Above: Director Lena Caron highlighted ivy with gold spray paint and wound it around a basic balsam wreath for a light, airy effect. Twigs and sprayed privet berries were tucked in as well.

old, I would retire to an office and remain seated at a desk for the rest of my years." Somehow, he never found time to put the second part of the plan into effect.

In the 1920s, Ladew visited Harford County, Maryland, with friends and discovered that it was ideally suited to fox hunting. In 1929 he bought Pleasant Valley Farm, where he established his home, his stables, and a garden. "I had always loved gardening," he wrote, "and, therefore, I decided that, though I would certainly make many mistakes, I would do the whole thing, including the landscaping, myself." Some forty years later, he had transformed 22 acres of rolling pasture into more than a dozen theme gardens linked by topiary. His achievements were recognized in May 1971 by the Garden Club of America with the Distinguished Service Medal, awarded for his "interest in developing and maintaining the most outstanding topiary garden in America, without professional help."

Ladew died in 1976 and left his house, furnishings, and property to a private foundation, which today administers the Ladew Topiary Gardens. From spring through fall, the main attraction is the gardens. But for three days in December the house itself is the focus of activity. That's when the staff and about 100 volunteers decorate the entire first floor for Christmas, using fresh greens, fruit, flowers, and lots of creativity.

Visitors begin lining up to tour the house about a half hour before the door opens, but

(continued on page 9)

Right: The fireplace is the only reminder that this room was originally the kitchen in the farmhouse that Ladew bought in 1929. A silver and magenta color scheme sparkles dramatically against the blue-green walls. Uschi Ostertag decorated the table with boxwood topiaries and a mixture of beaded, sprayed-silver, and real fruits and vegetables. Sprigs of boxwood tied to pinecones become place cards, and silver spray paint turns lace doilies into place mats. On the mantel, spray-painted artificial grapes and poinsettias enliven greenery arrangements.

6

A TOUCH OF SILVER

A touch of metallic spray paint can add glittering accents to decorations of fresh greenery and other natural materials. At Ladew, a hint of gold highlights the evergreens in the drawing room. In the dining room, silver transforms fruits, vegetables, vine wreaths, and artificial grapes and poinsettias.

Ordinary spray paint is easy to use, but always work in a well-ventilated room, or outdoors if possible. To paint craft foam, use acrylic polymer paints; enamels and lacquer-based paints will melt the material.

You can use the paint more efficiently and keep the spray from settling where you don't want it by placing the object to be sprayed in a box. Art students sometimes use a large box from which they remove the top and one side, creating a container that lets the vapor escape but confines the spray. Half of a refrigerator carton is ideal for this purpose.

Above: Give a fresh look to a vine wreath by attaching a small bunch of artificial grapes and a few stems of lavender. Then spray the whole decoration silver and add a bow for color.

Above: To make this tree, spray-paint the craft foam cone silver; then use a hot-glue gun to attach dried hydrangea. Dust the tree lightly with silver spray paint. Then add magenta bows tied to florists' picks.

Above: Ladew built this Adamesque library to accommodate an oval Chippendale "partner's desk" (so-called because it seats two). Robert A. Zimmerman, a member of the foundation's consulting committee, decorated the room in a southwest theme, with ristras *(strings of dried red peppers) between the bookcases and a tree trimmed with copper and gold bows, red peppers, and white lights. Metallic paper cord and wineberry (Rubus phoenicolasius), a prickly roadside bramble, wrap the tree loosely, creating a wildly free-form line.*

some people dash instead to the side lawn, where bunches of holly, boxwood, and magnolia are laid out for sale. In the studio below the house, wreaths, greenery arrangements, and topiary angels are sold almost as fast as volunteers can make them. Even those who buy only a ticket to tour the house come away with decorating ideas.

Ladew's house is furnished just as he left it—a comfortable, casual place filled with the personality of its gregarious owner. The noted interior designer Billy Baldwin, who was a good friend of Ladew, wrote in his autobiography that although Harvey was a New Yorker, he "rather fancied himself a born Southern colonel, and loved to surround himself with happy people. Some said that Harvey Ladew was hedonistic, but no one could deny that his guests enjoyed with him some of the happiest days of their lives."

9

Happy Holidays from Brer Rabbit and Friends

In the west parlor of the Wren's Nest, a story-teller recounts to an entranced audience the tale of "How Mr. Rabbit Lost His Fine Bushy Tail." The aroma of hot cider wafts from the dining room, and costumed volunteers dressed as Brer Rabbit and Brer Fox stroll through the house greeting visitors.

Christmas festivities are in full swing at the home of Joel Chandler Harris in Atlanta, Georgia. For the month of December, this museum house is decorated for the holidays and boasts a full calendar of events. And on the Sunday closest to December 9, visitors gather to join in the celebration marking the anniversary of Mr. Harris's birth.

Joel Chandler Harris, the author of the Uncle Remus tales, was a kind and gentle man. When a wren built her nest in his mailbox, he could not bring himself to have her removed and defied anyone to disturb her. His insistence that the family of birds not be bothered resulted in the name by which the house is still known.

Today, the Wren's Nest is owned and operated by the Joel Chandler Harris Association, whose purpose is to preserve the house and interpret the life and writings of the journalist and folklorist who lived here from 1881-1908. The house contains original furnishings as well as books, letters, and photographs that belonged to the Harris family. After studying the documents, the association has begun restoring the interior of the house to look just as it did in the late 1800s. The house is open throughout the year for storytelling sessions, special events, and tours.

A very special piece of artwork on display in the house is a wood sculpture (see photograph *opposite below*) which depicts Brer Fox escorting Brer Rabbit to jail on the charge of stealing vegetables. However, Brer Rabbit is slowly dropping the stolen vegetables as they walk along. By the time they reach the jail, the evidence will be nowhere in sight. The piece was created by a German wood-carver and presented to Mr. Harris as a gift in 1892.

Above: Two volunteers, dressed as Brer Fox and Brer Rabbit, greet guests during the Christmas open house at the Wren's Nest. The desk was in Mr. Harris's office at the Atlanta Constitution.

Above: The Wren's Nest in Atlanta, Georgia, looks much as it did when Joel Chandler Harris was in residence. The large porch was a favorite gathering place for the Harris family.

The story illustrated by the sculpture is not one that Mr. Harris wrote. Rather, the artist used his knowledge of the folktales and his own imagination to create the piece. It's just one example of the far-reaching influence and extensive popularity of the Uncle Remus tales. In the 1946 film *Song of the South,* Walt Disney drew on these stories to create his first feature film to mix animation and live action. That the Uncle Remus tales have enjoyed widespread fame is also evidenced by the fact that they have been published in many editions and translated into 27 languages.

Joel Chandler Harris's intention in publishing these folktales was to share the rich oral tradition of the African-American culture and to promote the unification of the different regions of the country. Uncle Remus first appeared as the narrator of dialect sketches in the *Atlanta Constitution* in 1876. Mr. Harris hoped that by recounting the folktales he had learned from former slaves he could help to heal the wounds of the Civil War.

According to Gil Watson, who has appeared in costume as Mr. Harris for 20 years, "Mr. Harris shared these stories to give us a simple truth: It didn't make much difference how big you were, or who you were, or what the odds were against you, if you used your head, you could come out ahead." The Uncle Remus tales are not as well-known today as in the past, but they still appeal to children, because of the witty tricks and intelligence that Brer Rabbit uses to triumph over Brer Fox.

Mr. Harris was a shy man and never sought the fame he achieved. Today, through the retelling of his famous tales, people are being entertained and exposed to a part of history. And there is something particularly appropriate to the Christmas season in Mr. Harris's message of peace and harmony.

Above right: Akbar Imhotep, storyteller-in-residence at the Wren's Nest, recounts the exciting tale of "How Mr. Rabbit Lost His Fine Bushy Tail" to a very attentive audience.

Above: Gil Watson sits in one of Harris's beloved rocking chairs. (Harris had one in almost every room of his house.) The wood sculpture beside the fireplace was inspired by the Uncle Remus tales.

Birmingham's Antebellum Home

Hostesses in hoop skirts, music filling the rooms with holiday cheer, goodies for visitors to savor—these samples of the Old South are only a few of those that guests are invited to experience at "Christmas at Arlington," a celebration held annually at the only remaining antebellum home in Birmingham, Alabama.

Sponsored by the Arlington Historical Association and the City of Birmingham, Arlington is lavishly decorated in December with the help of local floral designers. The highlight of the month is the opening weekend extravaganza, featuring holiday activities and musical performances by local pianists, choirs, handbell choirs, and quartets.

Arlington was built sometime after 1842 by William S. Mudd, a state representative and circuit court judge. It was purchased by the community in 1953. Today it houses a collection of furniture, paintings, porcelain, silver, and other decorative arts spanning a period of 100 years, with objects displayed in room settings. Tours focusing on architectural history and the decorative arts are offered, as well as special programs for children and students.

Above right: The only house museum in the city, Arlington typifies the Greek Revival style popular in the antebellum South.

Right: Vestavia Hills Girl Scout Troop 366 traditionally visits Arlington at Christmas. Members decorate trees for the birds and squirrels with ornaments made from seeds and fruit.

Opposite: Musicians fill the air with the sounds of the holidays during "Christmas at Arlington." Here a quartet entertains in the music room.

13

History by Candlelight In Houston

In the parlor, the Christmas tree sits decorated with paper fans, handcrafted ornaments, and crinkly ropes of foil, while in the kitchen, children are underfoot as mothers are busy preparing the Christmas feast. Scenes such as these of a 19th-century Christmas come alive each year with the Annual Candlelight Tour of Historic Sam Houston Park.

Located in downtown Houston, this turn-of-the-century park has evolved into an impressive summary of Texas history. One house was already on the site and five more were moved into the park from locations around Harris County. Together they represent the popular architecture and life-styles of the 1800s. A 100-year-old church and replicas of early Houston shops have also been added.

For 28 years, the Harris County Heritage Society has re-created holiday scenes in these houses and welcomed the public, free of charge. Volunteers research and decorate each home in an appropriate style.

The first house to be moved into the park was the Nichols-Rice-Cherry House, built in the 1840s. One of the last antebellum residences on the upper Gulf Coast of Texas, the house is a conservative Greek Revival design and was once home to William Marsh Rice, an

---

Above left: Nestled among skyscrapers in the middle of downtown Houston, St. John Church is a reverent reminder of the city's past. The church has had an active congregation for over 100 years.

Above right: The dining room in the Pillot House awaits the beginning of the Christmas dinner.

Right: The ornate and cluttered parlor of the Pillot House is typical of Victorian homes.

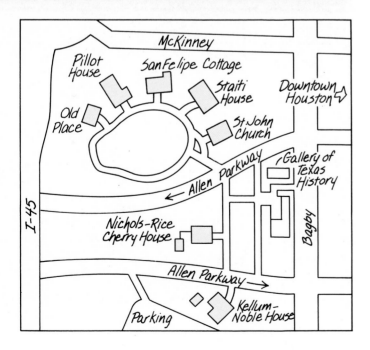

The putz, like the one shown here in San Felipe Cottage, was the pride of German families during the 19th century. This putz includes a manger scene, a house, a barn, a church, and an assortment of animals, not all in the same scale.

early Houston entrepreneur for whom Rice University was named. Each year, the Society re-enacts a ball at the house, based on Mrs. Rice's annual New Year's celebration. The ball is complete with reels, contra dancers, and period music. Elaborate clusters of fruit on the mantel and doors swagged with greens copy the Della Robbia style popular at the time.

Built in 1868, the Queen Anne-style Pillot House has been refurbished with guidance from authorities on Victoriana and reflects the comfortable life-style of the middle class. Cornucopias, gifts, and baskets of sweets hang on the Christmas tree, while the dining table is set and buffet laden with a Christmas feast.

The San Felipe Cottage, also dating to the late 1860s, represents Houston's German community. Here a *putz,* or expanded crèche, is arranged under a feather tree. This version of the Nativity scene includes figures of Mary, Joseph, and Baby Jesus, surrounded by miniature houses and barns, toys, carved animals, rocks, and moss.

St. John Church was built in 1891, although the original congregation was formed around 1860 by German and Swiss immigrants. German remained the primary language spoken in the church until the 1930s. Each year, the 120-year-old pump organ accompanies the Singing Boys of Houston.

The Annual Candlelight Tour takes place during the second weekend of December. Participants, warmed by cups of wassail, stroll down streets lit by hurricane lamps, while a host of choirs, musicians, and carolers fill the crisp night with sounds of Christmas.

Above right: A 19th-century ball is re-enacted each year in the Nichols-Rice-Cherry House to recall Margaret Rice's annual New Year's Eve celebration.

Right: Because fruit was such a luxury, only the wealthy could afford elaborate Della Robbia decorations such as this mantel centerpiece in the Nichols-Rice-Cherry house.

Savor the Season At Willow Oak

After a week of rain and low clouds, the sky finally clears just in time for the annual Christmas lecture and luncheon at Willow Oak Flower and Herb Farm in Severn, Maryland. Outdoors, the air is chilly, but inside the greenhouse it is warmer, and the room smells of cinnamon and dried herbs. Visitors sip a fragrant, golden-yellow herbal tea and nibble on *Christospomo*, a Greek Christmas bread. St. Nicholas, wearing a woolly beard, dispenses candy canes and snippets of history about the real St. Nicholas, a fourth-century bishop in Asia Minor. Then Maria Price, the owner of Willow Oak, moves to the table at the front of the greenhouse, and the program begins.

For the next hour, Maria relates the Christmas legends associated with various herbs and explains the ancient symbolism of evergreens. Then she leads the group through the woods to the barn, where the Snow Queen (alias Maria's mother, Aphrodite Poulos) tells the history of the crèche.

Lunch follows in Maria's house, which is decorated with wreaths and garlands of dried statice, roses, everlastings, and herbs. Everything on the menu, from the hot punch and appetizers to the soup, entrée, and sweets, is flavored with herbs from the farm.

Willow Oak, located just five miles south of the Baltimore-Washington International Airport, is a rural oasis in the midst of suburbia. There are horses, sheep, and chickens, a strip of woods, and twelve different gardens. Maria's grandparents bought the 40-acre property in the 1930s, and her grandmother, a native of Greece, grew vegetables, flowers, and herbs in the sandy soil. "She had a huge garden," recalls Maria. "I was always by her side, and I attribute a lot of my interest in gardening to her." Maria's education built on that interest. She has a bachelor's degree in biology and a master's in pharmacognosy, a branch of pharmacy that deals with the medicinal properties of plants.

Above: Hung with dried flowers and decorated with garlands, the greenhouse becomes a classroom for participants in the Christmas herbal lectures and luncheons at Willow Oak Flower and Herb Farm in Severn, Maryland.

Top: Maria Price shares the legends associated with Christmas plants.

18

The lecture-luncheons are offered seasonally during the year, and there are classes on growing herbs and using them in cooking and crafts. But the Christmas luncheons, held on the first three Saturdays of December, are the most popular. As many as 50 people attend each of the sessions, paying a modest fee that includes the meal. They can also shop in the greenhouse for plants, books, Willow Oak's own Christmas potpourri, and a wonderful variety of ornaments and decorations that Maria and her staff and family have created.

The luncheons began, she says, "as a nice way of presenting seasonal garden information. And people always seem to enjoy tasting something. It's more of an incentive to grow herbs if they can see how to use them."

Because Maria is always devising new crafts and recipes, a number of participants are regular visitors, especially at Christmas. "So many people make a point of starting the Christmas season by coming to the program," says Maria. "They tell us that it wouldn't be Christmas without coming here to get a little holiday spirit."

Top right: Resplendent in red velvet capes, Maria Price and a friend, Thea Khoeler, lead the group through the woods to the barn, where the Snow Queen (Maria's mother) explains the origins of the crèche and tells some of the folklore surrounding the animals at the manger.

Center right: The St. Nicholas ornament is made from spicy cinnamon dough, which is pressed into a cookie mold and then painted. Formed into a ring, the dough makes the wreath on the left, which is embellished with statice and tiny dried peppers. Kits for these two can be ordered from Willow Oak Flower and Herb Farm (see Resources, page 155). Lavender flowers, dried boxwood, and berries decorate the center wreath, made of ground lavender.

Bottom right: St. Nicholas's beard gets a last-minute adjustment before he enters the greenhouse to distribute his candy canes. The wool for the beard came from Maria's sheep.

Rockwood Revives
A Splendid Past

Christmas at Rockwood, in Wilmington, Delaware, is an Edwardian extravaganza, reproducing the way the holidays might have been celebrated in 1905, when the Bringhurst family lived here. Evergreen roping festoons the drawing room, where the Christmas-morning clutter of tissue paper, ribbons, and boxes suggests that the family has just finished opening presents. In the dining room, more roping, ribbons, and flowers create a festive setting for the holiday meal. From the entrance hall downstairs to the bedrooms upstairs, Rockwood reverberates with the life of an earlier era and of the individuals who lived here.

This Rural Gothic manor was built between 1851 and 1854 for Joseph Shipley, a merchant

Above and left: On Christmas morning, 1905, the Bringhurst family would find gifts hidden around the room and on the tree.

21

Above: A Victorian-style motto, made of dried flowers and seed pods, hangs in the conservatory.

banker from Wilmington who spent his working life in England. At age 50, he decided to retire and returned to Delaware to build Rockwood, where he lived until his death in 1867. The estate passed to his two maiden sisters, and after they died, it was auctioned and the proceeds divided among the seven principal heirs. One of them, Sarah Shipley Bringhurst, bought the house, grounds, and some of the furnishings and presented them to her son, Edward, Jr., and his wife, Anna.

Edward and Anna were already middle-aged when they moved to the estate in 1892. Three of their four children came with them: Mary,

age 27, Edith, 18, and Edward III, 8. The eldest daughter, Elizabeth (Bessie), had married an Irish textile merchant in 1886 and was living at Kilwaughter Castle in Ireland. But she maintained close ties to her family through a constant exchange of letters.

Those letters, thousands of photographs taken by Edward III, and a wealth of other documents have allowed curator Rebecca Hammell to reconstruct a detailed picture of life at Rockwood between 1892 and 1920. The Christmas decorations are based on family photographs that show pine roping draped from the chandeliers to cornices throughout

22

Above: The dining room is decorated for the Bringhurst family's Christmas dinner. Place cards rest against English crackers (cardboard tubes that contain a paper hat, a proverb, and a small gift).

Above: This desk belonged to Bessie Bringhurst Galt-Smith, who was living in Ireland at Kilwaughter Castle when her parents moved into Rockwood. Later, Bessie joined her family there.

the house. In the drawing room Hammell re-creates a custom described by Bessie when she was still in Ireland: "Mrs. Paris and Rose [the housekeeper and head housemaid] had tied [strings] to our presents, and then taken [them] up stairs and down stairs & hither & yon, & then brought all the ends into the oak hall with a tag on the end. Such a time as we had unraveling the tangle! . . . We were two hours finding everything, and they were most splendidly arranged. Sometimes they knotted two of the ends together, when about 1/2 way, & then we had to stop and untie them before we could go on."

Letters also recorded the kinds of gifts that family members exchanged, and Rockwood's drawing room is strewn with typical items, such as photograph albums, silk stockings, and gloves. The Christmas tree reflects the documented Victorian practice of decorating with paper ornaments, pressed-tin stars and animals, fruit, and bags of candy. There would also have been gifts: calendars might be propped among the branches, and small presents in boxes wrapped with tissue and ribbon would be hung on the tree for distribution on Christmas morning.

After her husband's death, Bessie returned to Delaware and joined her mother, sister Mary, and brother at Rockwood. All four were aging, says Hammell, "but life was not dull, and through the 1920s, they entertained and traveled." Mary even made home movies of her adventures in North Africa and Arabia.

Mary died in 1965 at the age of 100, leaving Rockwood to her favorite niece, and in 1974, New Castle County received the property to run as a museum. Now educational and community activities go on year-round, culminating in Christmas. The decorations go up in mid-November, and on four evenings in December, costumed actors present a short skit about the family and servants on Christmas Eve, 1905. The atmosphere is so festive and lively that visitors cannot help but be inspired to rush home and deck their own halls.

24

Holiday Traditions

This Collector Is Surrounded by A Host of Angels

"In difficult moments, I have felt I was borne on the wings of angels," Deen Day Smith says. "This feeling of support has gotten me through some hard times." That's why at Christmas, angels are one of her favorite decorations. For the holidays, Deen decorates her home in Duluth, Georgia, with angels, butterflies, and nature's bounty. She is an ardent gardener and a gifted floral designer, and she uses her artistic talents to showcase an array of angels. They are the focal point of arrangements of garden greenery, as well as tree ornaments and package toppers. Her collection includes ceramic figures, reproductions of baroque angels from the Metropolitan Museum of Art, and Victorian paper angels.

Deen also uses butterfly ornaments in her holiday decorating. The butterfly is a traditional symbol of eternal life and the resurrection of Christ. "Butterflies represent the metamorphosis that comes through faith. We don't know what will come after this life, but it will be wonderful," she says. "My first husband began my collection of butterflies because this metamorphosis was very important to him." Deen was instrumental in the development of the Cecil B. Day Butterfly Center at Callaway Gardens, which is named in honor of her late husband and grew out of their fascination with butterflies.

Deen's angels and butterflies reflect her faith in God and serve as reminders of the true meaning of Christmas. As she says, "Christmas is a busy and joyous time, but most important, it is the celebration of Christ's birth."

Above: Deen Day Smith uses angels throughout her home at Christmas. Her collections of angels and butterflies are one of the ways she expresses her strong Christian faith. Here she is shown in front of her angel-bedecked tree with some of her angelic wraps and a gold lamé angel on a deep red pillow.

Above left: Deen commissioned a pair of bronze angels to decorate her dining room table. Each holds a bowl in outstretched hands to contain an arrangement.

Above: Deen collects angels and other holiday decorations on her travels. The ornaments on her tree include a ceramic Madonna and child, Victorian-style paper angels, a fabric butterfly with gold details, and an angel dressed in a coarsely woven golden robe.

Top: Placing an angel atop a candelabra is one of the unusual ways that Deen displays her collection. The small cherubs on the table are the work of a Spanish wood-carver.

A Caring Custom At Ten Mile House

On Stage Coach Road, not far from downtown Little Rock, stands Ten Mile House. Arkansas was still frontier territory when this structure was built in the late 1820s or early 1830s, with bricks made on the premises. The center hall has 16-inch-thick plaster walls and cypress-plank floors, and a banister of black walnut curves up the stair to the attic.

Every December owner Nancy Newel and her friends decorate Ten Mile House and welcome the public. Proceeds from the open house benefit a charity that's especially poignant at Christmastime, the Pulaski County SCAN (Suspected Child Abuse and Neglect).

Nancy began hosting the fund-raiser because, she says, "For me, Christmas is a time for taking note of what you have and what you can do to help the less fortunate. SCAN is a private agency that works statewide with families having problems, and at Christmastime, it

Above right: The Arkansas frontier-style home was built with bricks made on the premises by slaves and has eight fireplaces, including two in the kitchen. Massive twin chimneys at each end of the house give it a solid, fortresslike appearance.

Right: Nancy's son, Brett, looks on as Nancy feeds Dolly, an angora goat. Their menagerie also includes chickens, ducks, pheasants, turkeys, peacocks, a rabbit, a sheep, a dog, and a cat.

Opposite: A black walnut banister leads to the central hall, where antique toys and folk art enhance Nancy's Christmas ornament collection. Greenery and fruit garland the door and chandelier.

Opposite above: In Brett's bedroom, a tabletop tree rests on a European tile cookstove, one of Nancy's early antique acquisitions.

takes care of a lot of children. I wanted to help." Sharing Ten Mile House offered a way.

Her home's name refers to the house's distance from the center of Little Rock. Since the homestead fronted the southwest stagecoach trail to Texas, it served as a stopping place for travelers to water their horses and sometimes stay the night. During the Civil War, Union troops occupied the house. In an upstairs bedroom, missing chunks of plaster along concentric rings still record the accuracy of soldiers taking target practice.

Nancy has researched this history in depth in the course of restoring the house. And from the beginning, she has worked with leading architects, preservationists, and historians to plan each phase of restoration. From picket fences to replaced hardware, everything at Ten Mile House is being done as authentically as possible. Nancy sees herself as the custodian of a part of Arkansas's heritage. She doesn't even dig a rose bed without calling in the state archaeologist, who excavates the area first to look for artifacts.

Opening the house to the community at Christmas is another way for Nancy to express her sense of stewardship of the homestead's history. And what better time to revive the Ten Mile tradition of hospitality than the Christmas season?

Above left and left: Boxwood garland and sumac frame English Staffordshire figurines on the mantel. Flanking the fireplace below, black urns hold topiary standards made of boxwood, dried hydrangea, apples, cranberry garlands, grapevine, and cranberry-colored velvet ribbon.

Opposite: Each December, Nancy Newell opens the doors of Ten Mile House for an open house to benefit SCAN (Suspected Child Abuse and Neglect), a statewide organization that works to help families overcome their problems.

Folk Art That Comes From the Heart

"To me, kindness is the river life flows on," says Carl Pendergrass. He's sitting in the kitchen of his Chattanooga home, and just behind him is the workshop where he and his wife, Lynn, fashion the dolls and doll-sized chairs that have become their sideline business.

As they talk about their experiences as artisans, they focus again and again on the people they've come in contact with and how enriching those relationships have been. Carl is a postal worker. Lynn works in a discount department store. But for several years now, they've put their creative energy into Rag Bag Loveys.

It began when Lynn made a Father Christmas doll, entered it in a contest, and won. She then began making more dolls as gifts for family. "I didn't realize how much I would like

Above right: Lynn's little dolls link hands and draw a wide smile across the Pendergrasses' mantel. Above them, her nature-loving Father Christmas is poised to feed the birds.

Right: Lynn and Carl Pendergrass's studio is just off the kitchen in their home in Chattanooga, Tennessee. Here they make the dolls, small chairs, and portrait chairs like the one Carl is holding. All are sold under the name Rag Bag Loveys.

Opposite: A Santa Lucia angel doll, an old Father Christmas, and a Lilliputian rocker are three examples of the Pendergrasses' art. Their work has been featured in national magazines and is sold in the gift shops of the Smithsonian Institution and the American Folk Art Museum.

33

Above: Lighting his way with a lantern, Father Christmas waves the stars and stripes and carries a chamois bag filled with toys and treats. Rabbit fur trims his velvet robe.

Above: Lynn and Carl collaborated to create one of Santa's industrious helpers, who works away at a bench cluttered with trinkets. Carl used an old pocket watch for the face on the grandfather clock.

it," she says. Part of the pleasure comes from inventing variations. Some of her Father Christmases wave flags and hold lanterns. Some carry birdhouses and bags of seed, and some, having completed the annual rounds, stretch out for a nap or read a newspaper while soaking their feet.

Carl helped by making many of the accessories for the dolls, carving scissors, toys, pipes, and other items from wood. Then he decided to make chairs for them. The diminutive folk art creations took off.

What Lynn and Carl most enjoy is making things for people who have special requests. Particularly popular are their portrait dolls and chairs. Sometimes, for example, women bring pictures of their granddaughters to Lynn, who makes a doll wearing the same kind of dress

and resembling the little girl, but with the face rendered in Lynn's distinctive style.

Lynn paints the faces for Carl's portrait chairs, as well. He says, "I've always liked people and enjoy being around them. I wish I could capture people in a way that would show others what I see. That's what's so special about what Lynn does."

Their mutual respect and affection comes through clearly, especially when you see them in the workshop where, side by side, they collaborate and inspire each other with new folk art creations. Carl sums it up simply: "Life has been very good to us." And that peaceful happiness shines from each Father Christmas and each chair made of hearts.

(For information on ordering Rag Bag Loveys, see Resources on page 155.)

Focus on Traditions:
Keeping Christmas in Kentucky

Every family observes traditions during the holidays, whether it's attending Mass on Christmas Eve, gathering with kinfolk at Grandma's for a midday feast, or dusting off old family movies from years past to watch. On the following pages, you'll find stories about four families in Louisville, Kentucky, and the special ways they choose to celebrate the season. A little out of the ordinary but clearly a lot of fun, these customs will, we hope, inspire you to revive old traditions or create new ones of your own.

Above: Just like ships of old, the Christmas ship twinkles through the night, laden with gifts for those who patiently await its arrival.

SAILING THROUGH THE HOLIDAYS

Virginia Woodward and her family sail through Christmas on a ship that's four feet tall and four feet wide with three silver lamé sails and a glossy red hull full of presents. This unusual tradition—decking a ship—began with Virginia's great-grandfather, who fashioned the first ship out of a washtub.

No one is exactly sure where the idea came from. "My great-grandfather claimed there were sailing captains in our family, and on Christmas Day he would always sing 'I Saw Three Ships Come Sailing In,' " says Virginia. "But I think that during cost-conscious times, the family adapted by putting a broom handle into an old washtub, hoping that 'some day our ship would come in.' "

The original ship was refined by Virginia's grandfather, who built an elaborate eighteen-mast rigger. After her grandmother vowed never to make eighteen sails again, he made the current ship with only three sails.

Virginia's grandmother decorated the ship each year, using a certain theme. "When I was a little girl, I could hardly contain myself until we got to Grandmother's because it was a big secret," Virginia reminisces. Themes have included "The Owl and the Pussycat" with a pea green boat and *Peter Pan,* with Captain Hook staunchly positioned at the stern.

Although Virginia and her family no longer use a theme for the ship, they still decorate it with some of the original ornaments. And as for Virginia's son, Bubba—a Christmas *tree* at his house would be an oddity because he has always had a Christmas ship.

THE TREE OF
OUR TRAVELS

Each year, Ann Stewart Anderson and her husband, Ron Mikulak, celebrate Christmas by riding camels in Egypt, basking on sun-drenched beaches on the coast of St. Croix, and attending bullfights in Seville, Spain. They accomplish this holiday globe-trotting without ever leaving home, simply by decorating their tree with souvenirs from their travels.

"What wonderful memories we have of our trips!" Ann says. "Each year when we take out the ornaments, we not only remember past Christmases but also all of the vacations we have taken." Because Ann has always loved to travel, she decided that collecting souvenirs would be an interesting way to decorate her Christmas tree. "In fact, I think my souvenir-covered tree was one of the first things about me my husband was attracted to!" she says.

Above: A miniature gondolier's hat from Venice; a delicate, filigreed boat from Portugal; clothespin people from Canterbury, England; and an ornate shoe from Istanbul are among the many ornaments on Ann and Ron's tree. The paper Eiffel Tower is one they assembled themselves.

The couple's unique collection now consists of about 50 ornaments, ranging from a minia-ture gondolier's hat from Venice to a tiny Memphis guitar. They have also expanded this tradition to their Nativity scene, which in-cludes a camel from Egypt, a burro from Santa Fe, and a warthog from Africa.

When traveling, Ann and Ron search for just the right souvenir, and they don't neces-sarily make the most obvious selection. They also prize handcrafted souvenirs and those that they can assemble themselves at home, such as their Eiffel Tower. "The challenge to keep searching for certain items has become part of the fun in traveling," Ann says, "and that adds to the pleasure of our vacations."

Above: Ann and Ron scout for unique souvenirs on each trip, not only for their tree, but also for their Nativity.

LIVING IN A
WONDERLAND OF TOYS

Whenever Santa is running behind schedule or has a particularly hard order to fill, he calls on his old friends, Dr. William Furnish and his wife, Mary, for last-minute help. After all, with a house literally filled with toys in every nook and cranny from the basement to the third floor, who is better equipped to rescue Santa when he's in a bind?

"Our collection can be quite overwhelming in some ways," Dr. Furnish explains, "because it's like celebrating Christmas all year round. Most decorators use toys as accent pieces, but with this weird way that we live, the toys here at our home have taken over."

The Furnishes have one of the foremost toy collections in the region, with four or five hundred electric and steam engine train sets, dozens of dolls, books, puzzles, dollhouses, and airplanes, plus everything in-between. "Anything that can be played with or that is just plain amusing is considered a toy," William insists.

With thousands of pieces in storage and many on loan to museums, an extensive cataloging system is required to keep up with such a large collection. There are Santas parachuting and airplanes flying from antlers mounted on the wall, a complete marionette stage with puppets set up behind the sitting room sofa, and, in the kitchen, a glass showcase full of small wonders that doubles as a work island. Some of the most surprising pieces are a 10-foot psychedelic pterodactyl suspended from the ceiling and an 1810 automated bone carving of dancing men, made by French prisoners in the Napoleonic Wars.

But old friends are still their favorites. Stashed under a 75-year-old German feather tree, William's very first, are his Santa-on-a-goose rattle and Mary's Raggedy Ann and Andy. A celluloid camel rests close by. William says, "I looked for this camel for 52 years. The

Above: Seated amid a small portion of their collection on the third floor, the Furnishes proudly show a few of their old favorites.

kid next door had one when I was small, and I was envious." Camels and other Egyptian artifacts became popular after King Tut's tomb was opened in 1926.

With a Santa-like twinkle in his eyes and tufts of white hair that accentuate his rosy complexion, William claims he has carried his passion for toys with him from childhood. "I began collecting as an infant, when my very first rattle was laid beside me in my crib," he says with a grin. "Now we're receiving toys from our *grandchildren* for Christmas!"

Yet William contends that their compulsion for preserving the past is not always an advantage. "Because of the time and space involved, we think the most fortunate people are those who collect nothing at all," he chuckles. There's probably at least one round-bellied fellow who would beg to differ!

A PUZZLING CHRISTMAS

The tree has been trimmed, the presents have been wrapped, and the stockings have been hung by the chimney with care. Yet Lane Adams can't lie snug in her bed until all eight of her Christmas puzzles are worked. So, with the help of 35 to 50 friends who annually congregate for Lane's puzzle party, all 8,000 pieces find their places before Santa's yearly visit, giving Lane holiday peace of mind.

"The tradition began 10 years ago with our first two puzzles, both with 1,000 pieces," Lane remembers. "When we obviously weren't going to finish before Christmas, we invited neighbors over to help us. It was so much fun, we've just continued doing it every year since—without ever losing a puzzle piece!"

Although the party originated with a few people in the neighborhood, it soon grew to include close family friends and school buddies of Lane's four children. The number of puzzles to work also grew—from two to eight.

"The most puzzles we have worked in one night is eight, and I think that might be the limit. But as I continue to find new puzzles and receive them as gifts, I will rotate them from year to year."

In addition to starting each puzzle around the edges so that guests aren't overwhelmed when they first arrive, Lane also prepares a buffet for her puzzle-working pals. The feast includes a variety of meats, homemade rolls, beaten biscuits, and assorted holiday appetizers and sweets.

Such a spread contributes to keeping the Christmas spirit alive throughout the night. "Almost everyone stays until the puzzles are done," Lane says, "and sometimes that can be as late as 4:00 a.m. But we have great fun visiting with friends and family, so the time passes quickly. And in the end, we complete each and every puzzle. Besides, who wants to work Christmas puzzles after Christmas?"

Above: With plenty of punch and goodies to fuel their creative energies, guests of all ages huddle together to complete the puzzles. Hostess Lane Adams (fifth from left) moves from one table to the next, offering a helping hand.

Above: Although they might be a bit "puzzled" at first, it doesn't take long for Margaret White and Anne Lindsay to become absorbed in finding the right place for each of the pieces. Both have attended Lane's puzzle party for the last seven years.

Making Time For Friends

Even before guests reach the door of Patricia Maxwell's house in Athens, Georgia, they can hear the laughter from inside. Between 10:00 a.m. and noon, at least 70 people will stop by to exchange Christmas greetings and sample some of the goodies that Patricia and her friend Carol Driver have prepared. (One of their most popular recipes is below.)

"Athens is a close-knit, loving town," says Carol, "but as everywhere, the holidays can be hectic." Several years ago, she and Patricia decided that the best way to see as many people as possible was to hold a mid-morning coffee. Friends could drop in for a few minutes or for an hour, according to their schedules. It was such a success that it became an annual event. Dropping in and out can be easier said than done, however. Says one guest, "I start talking and I just can't leave."

Above: To make sure they see as many friends as possible at Christmas, Carol Driver (third from left) and Patricia Maxwell (far right) co-host a drop-in coffee every year. It's held on a weekday morning so that guests can stop by on their lunch hour or take a break from shopping.

VEGGIE BARS

- 2 (8-ounce) cans refrigerated crescent dinner rolls
- 2 (8-ounce) packages cream cheese, softened
- ¼ cup mayonnaise or salad dressing
- 1 (1-ounce) envelope ranch-style salad dressing mix
- 1 medium-size sweet red pepper, chopped
- 1 medium-size green pepper, chopped
- ¾ cup (3 ounces) shredded Cheddar cheese
- ½ cup coarsely chopped broccoli flowerets
- ½ cup coarsely chopped fresh mushrooms

Unroll crescent roll dough. Place in a lightly greased 15- x 10- x 1-inch jellyroll pan, pressing edges and perforations together to line bottom of pan. Bake at 350° for 7 to 8 minutes or until browned. Cool.

Combine cream cheese, mayonnaise, and salad dressing mix; beat at medium speed of an electric mixer 1 minute or until smooth. Spread over crust in pan. Combine peppers and remaining ingredients; sprinkle over cream cheese mixture. Cover and chill 8 hours. Cut into 1¼-inch squares. Yield: 8 dozen.

A House Full of Handcrafts

One look inside Martha Elliott-Woodard's home in Chesapeake, Virginia, is all you need to know that she adores handcrafts of all kinds. Each room is filled with pieces of folk and primitive art, the works of other craftspeople and her own creations. From pine swags embellished with cinnamon-dough ornaments and slices of dried fruit to displays of feather trees and whimsical wooden Santas, examples of Martha's creative talents and Christmas spirit are everywhere.

Martha has been a craftswoman for 18 years. She does all kinds of crafts, but mostly she works in wood. "My signature item is my Belsnickel (from the German *Pelznickel,* which means 'St. Nicholas in fur'), but I also paint primitives and make wooden gameboards, shorebirds, animals, birdhouses, and watermelons," she says. Martha thinks her early childhood has inspired some of her work. "I lived on a truck farm as a child, and a lot of the colors I use in my crafts come from my memories of that farm."

Martha adds, "I love the old-world look and anything German, and my work clearly shows these influences. Also, I have always been fascinated with Santas from different countries and traditions." Each of Martha's Belsnickels and Father Christmases (English-style Santas) is one of a kind.

"The Santas are a lot of fun to carve and dress because there is no limit to what I can do. I buy old clothes at flea markets and thrift

Above: Martha Elliott-Woodard is an accomplished craftswoman. She is shown here in her Chesapeake, Virginia, home with one of her English-style Father Christmas figures.

Above left: The mantel showcases some of the many Santas and feather trees in Martha's folk art collection. Quilted stockings and a pair of antique ice skates hang beside a garland made of bay leaves, cinnamon sticks, pomegranates, and dried apple slices. A tobacco stick suspended beneath the mantel displays hand-dipped candles.

Above: Cinnamon-dough ornaments hang from the pine garland draped on the kitchen light fixture. Martha grouped an old birdhouse with a grapevine tree decked with egg and bird ornaments and natural materials to dress up one corner of her kitchen. Martha also enjoys cooking, and home-baked goodies are an important part of her holiday celebration.

Above: The tree in the den is decorated with handmade ornaments and natural materials. Crocheted snow-flakes, beeswax hearts, twig stars, and tiny quilted ornaments hang alongside cotton bolls, dried pomegranates, and dried orange and apple slices. Martha uses rough twine hangers to blend with the natural look of the ornaments. A collection of old toys and teddy bears surrounds the base of the tree.

shops and re-make them to dress the wooden figures," she explains. Each figure features a delicately carved face with painted details and a long, white beard, and each bulging sack is full of tiny handcrafted toys. "I make most of the toys that go in the sack from old quilts," she says, "but I also try to put in at least one old or antique toy."

At Christmas, Martha's home is filled with her handiwork. She crafted most of the ornaments that hang on the tree in the den, which is surrounded by a collection of old toys and teddy bears. "I crocheted some snowflakes in white thread and had to do them over in ecru because the white was too stark," she chuckles. Dried orange and apple slices are used as ornaments, as are cotton bolls and dried pomegranates. Stars, hearts, and other cookie cutter shapes made of cinnamon dough add a touch of holiday spice to the tree and other arrangements around the house.

Other decorations in her home include a variety of folk art Santas, lining the mantel and standing on tabletops and cupboards. Martha's Father Christmases and Belsnickels are displayed in places of honor. And in the kitchen, a grapevine tree decorated with bird and egg ornaments, white lights, Spanish moss, and eucalyptus is grouped with an old birdhouse and arranged in front of a large window.

Martha's folk art collections and handmade items bring the atmosphere of a simpler time to her home. As Martha says, "Primitives are warm, cozy, and comforting. It's nice to leave the hustle and bustle and come home to a different era—you step back in time when you come through my door." As she sits surrounded by her wonderful collections, with Christmas just around the corner, the hustle and bustle of the outside world is very far away indeed. (To contact Martha about her work, see Resources on page 155.)

A GARLAND FROM THE KITCHEN

Combine bay leaves and cinnamon sticks for a garland that decorates the mantel and lightly scents the room. To make this garland, you will need dry (but not brittle) bay leaves, cinnamon sticks, dried pomegranates, and dried apple slices.

According to Martha, the best way to dry fruit slices is to use the oven to remove most of the moisture. Cut each apple into very thin crosswise slices. Arrange the slices in one layer on a wire rack and bake in an oven at the lowest possible temperature for two hours. Remove the apple slices from the oven and let sit at room temperature until completely dry. Dry orange slices in the same manner, except bake them in the oven for eight to 10 hours.

With a very small drill bit, drill a hole through the center of each cinnamon stick and

through the top (or smallest part) of each pomegranate. Use a large-eyed embroidery needle and 18-pound squid line (available in most hardware stores) or 10-pound monofilament to string bay leaves, cinnamon sticks, pomegranates, and apple slices, as desired. If carefully handled and stored, the garland will last several years.

Above: Inside Santa's Workshop, temporarily set up in the lobby of the Hill-Haven nursing home in Louisville, resident Helen Oechslin answers an incoming telephone call from a hopeful child. Beside her, Stefanie Kaiser sits on the lap of Santa (employee Greg Hardin).

Ho Ho Hotline—Santa Is Only a Call Away

There once was a time when the only way to get in touch with Santa was to write letters of Christmas requests and reassurances of good behavior. Now, instead of scrounging around for pencil and paper, all kids have to do to reach Santa is pick up the telephone.

Every December, a special telephone line is installed at each Hill-Haven Nursing Home across the country. Operated by employees and residents, the Ho Ho Hotline allows local children to speak directly to Santa or Mrs. Claus. For two weeks before Christmas, these volunteers field calls from wishful girls and boys. Then, for the two days after Christmas, the "Ho Ho Thank-you Line" is open, giving youngsters a chance to thank Santa. Now into its 11th year, this holiday tradition serves two good purposes. Besides putting children in touch with Santa, the hotline allows nursing home residents to be busy and productive at a time when feelings of isolation are typically the highest.

In Louisville, Kentucky, activity director Kim Pearson not only oversees the local hotline at the nursing home; she also creates a Santa's Workshop where children can come and visit Mr. and Mrs. Claus. "The employees and residents have such a good time dressing up and visiting with the children," she says.

Kim requires volunteers to attend a Ho Ho Academy that prepares them to answer the hotline as Santa or Mrs. Claus. "They learn what kinds of questions to expect and what answers might be given," she explains.

In addition to using the local hot-line numbers, children can also place calls through the free long distance number—1-800-422-XMAS—during December.

Decorating for the Holidays

Above: Tina Hayward uses American flags on the tree in the family room to unify a motley collection of ornaments that Laird (left) and Brad (right) help her hang. Patriotic folk art that is normally displayed elsewhere around the house is also gathered around the tree for Christmas. Tina's grandmother made the cloth doll that Laird is holding, and her grandfather carved the George Washington doll near his foot.

Decking the Halls With a Personal Touch

For Tina Hayward of Greenville, Delaware, Christmas decorating is an annual opportunity to be creative. "I do something different every year," she says. "I start in August, looking at Christmas books and holiday issues of decorating magazines that I've saved, to get ideas." She packs these resources away separately every year so that she can pull them out and leaf through them for inspiration. "I like to go on holiday house tours, too," she adds, "to see what other people are doing, even if it's not something I would do."

Last year, when these pictures were taken, Tina and her husband, Pierre duPont Hayward, had just been on the receiving end of such a pilgrimage, having lent their home to a house tour. But a visitor gets the impression that Tina would take just as much trouble with the decorations even if the family weren't expecting hundreds of people.

Sometimes her ideas become traditions. The tree in the family room, for example, has always been decorated with a miscellany of ornaments—sturdy ones her sons, Laird, 7, and Brad, 5, could hang; pictures of the children in Christmassy frames; handmade items; and ornaments that reflect the family's interests.

Several years ago—before the idea appeared in magazines and books—she decided to use American flags on the tree to "pull it all together," she explains. The family liked it so well that the flags are now customary. And for the holidays, she brings her collection of patriotic folk art from other rooms and displays it under the tree to reinforce the theme. In 1990, the motif took on special meaning, she adds, because both her brother and her sister-in-law had been called up to serve in the Persian Gulf.

Creatively recombining things she and Pierre already have is one of the ways Tina makes decorating easy, and it gives a fresh look to objects that the family lives with all year.

Above: A fox collection sets the theme in the den. Pinecone lights, red and natural-colored raffia, branches of fresh white pine, and eucalyptus pods decorate the artificial tree.

47

Above: Baskets that stay on the counter year-round to hold bread, fruit, and snacks are embellished with silk poinsettias and fresh greenery. (Even the snacks are in Christmas colors, with red and green candy!) Tina also tucks small potted poinsettias into decorative tins for spots of seasonal color.

In the kitchen, baskets that are normally clustered on the counter to hold fruit, bread, and snacks are embellished with branches of greenery and berries for the holidays. Small poinsettias enhance the effect. To give the live plants a more appealing presentation, she tucks the pots into reproduction antique tins.

In the den, foxes and fox-hunting set the theme. Tina says that, as a girl, she used to hunt, so her father began giving her jewelry with fox motifs. Later, when she taught school, she wore one of those pieces of jewelry every day. Soon her students were bringing her fox figurines and trinkets as Christmas gifts. From these beginnings her collection grew, and at Christmas she puts everything on display, including an array of stuffed animals around the base of an artificial tree. To add softer texture and a more natural look to the tree, Tina tucks in branches of fresh white pine and eucalyptus pods. She also garlands the tree with raffia, which adds a loose, gestural line.

Brass coaching horns allude to the hunting and horseback riding theme, and frosted-glass pinecone lights give a sophisticated twist to the natural materials.

The living room is formal, and its decorations are spectacular. Artificial topiaries with white lights and wire-edged ribbons frame the portrait above the mantel. To provide transition from the topiary to the mantel, Tina flanks each with a dracaena and a pineapple, paired for their similarly spiky foliage. A big frilly head of ornamental kale hides each dracaena's pot. The kale, dusty miller, and greenery come from the Haywards' garden, and Tina simply places them on the mantel along with pomegranates, protea, and lady apples. "I keep the kale in the refrigerator or out in the barn until right before the party," she says. "If it's in a warm room for a long time, it starts to smell cabbagey."

Tina comes by her creativity naturally. Her grandparents made some of the folk art dolls under the family room tree, her father worked in wood, and her mother has a flair for making celebrations special. She started ornament collections for each of her children, recalls Tina. "We got an ornament every year, and my mother would write the date and our initials on each one." Now Tina has started similar collections for Laird and Brad.

She also devises special wrapping paper for each person on her list—paper stamped with a Chinese dragon design for her aunt, cats for her mother-in-law, trains for one son, and dinosaurs for the other. She started custom-designing wrappings before Brad and Laird could read, so they could tell their gifts apart. Now it's a way of adding something special to gifts for each person in the family. What makes her go to such lengths? "I just love Christmas," she says. "Who doesn't?"

Opposite: In the living room, Tina creates a lavish mantel using potted plants, artificial topiaries, gold lamé bows, and ornamental kale and dusty miller from her garden.

Six Ways to Say Welcome

When you decorate the outside of your house, you extend a Christmas greeting to all passersby. And the time and creativity you and your neighbors put into outdoor decorations are like a gift to each other, creating a holiday spirit that's contagious.

The six decorations shown here offer a variety of ideas for putting on a festive face. An arrangement of fruit, branches, and greenery under a carriage lamp (*left*) makes a spectacular splash. It is built on a foundation of craft foam that has been covered with chicken wire to keep it from splitting. The craft foam is then wired to the base of the lamp. The lowest pinecones are secured with monofilament so that they will drape down the wall; then boughs of silver fir and juniper are inserted to make a generous spray. Lichen-covered hickory branches, winterberry, possum haw, and other berries are added for an airy, linear effect around the lamp. Lady apples, yellow apples, and pomegranates on florists' picks go in last, along with the remaining pinecones.

For a more understated arrangement of fruit and greenery, assemble a badge to hang beside the door (*right*). This one also starts with a craft foam base. Because the pineapple will make the badge heavy, you'll need to wrap florists' wire around the craft foam block as if you were wrapping a package with ribbon; then wrap another wire around the point where they cross to make a hook for hanging. Secure the pineapple first, using florists' picks. Then add greenery and red bows around it to complete the spray.

If you have garden ornaments along your walk or flanking the front door, dress them up for the holidays. A stone garden statue from England offers a winsome greeting (see page 52). The dog holds a basket, so the florist simply arranged flowers in a plastic pot and placed them in this container.

For a traditional welcome that's quick and easy, try twin wreaths like those shown on page 52. Start with purchased wreaths of fresh fir and use a hot-glue gun to attach pinecones and bunches of holly berries. Wire artificial grapes to hang in the center of each wreath and add a puffy bow of paper-twist ribbon.

An arrangement of apples, magnolia leaves, and Spanish moss under the window of a home in Williamsburg, Virginia, turns the traditional apple fan upside down (see page 53). To create a window decoration like this, you'll need to cut a half-ellipse from ½-inch-thick plywood. The long edge should be about the

51

width of your window; the depth at the center should be a little more than one-third of the length. Paint the wood dark green so that it will blend with the foliage. Then hammer finishing nails into the plywood (see sketch). Use a staple gun to attach magnolia leaves and boxwood around the edges of the fan. Push the apples onto the nails and tuck Spanish moss around the apples to hide the base.

Fruit is the usual companion to greenery for Christmas decorations, but for a whimsical alternative, use vegetables. The generous wreath below, made of white pine, fir, and juniper, is starred with garlic, brussels sprouts, radishes, and scallions, all inserted with florists' picks. It's the perfect way for a gourmet cook to say Merry Christmas!

Left, below left, and below right: Make your entry distinctive. Dress up a garden statue with flowers or decorate ordinary wreaths with vegetables or grapes and paper bows.

A WILLIAMSBURG
WINDOW DRESSING

To make the apple fan above, hammer finishing nails 2 to 3 inches from the outer edge of the fan shape along the curve, driving them in at an upward angle and spacing them 3½ to 4 inches apart. Position the second row of nails about 4 inches from the first. Use screw eyes and hooks to hang the apple fan.

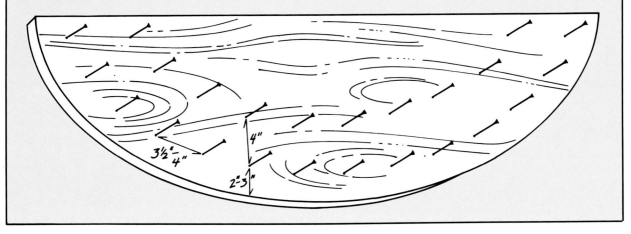

Sensational Centerpieces

Sitting down to a holiday feast is one of the highlights of the season, and part of what makes the meal special is the tablescape you create as a setting. When you bring out the best china and silver and assemble a special centerpiece, you declare that it's an occasion for celebration. Here are four ideas to inspire you this year.

The traditional Williamsburg-style S-swag *(opposite)* conveys generosity and abundance.

To make it, cut a 20-inch craft foam wreath in half and position the halves on the table to form an S. (To protect the table, cut a piece of heavy plastic, such as an old shower curtain or a garbage bag, to the same S-shape and place it under the craft foam.) Connect the halves with a pineapple secured with florists' picks. Then use florists' picks to insert lady apples, yellow and red apples, red pears, and osage oranges along the top of the form. Next, wire sprigs of boxwood to florists' picks and insert them at a slight angle to cover the craft foam. The boxwood should be 3 to 4 inches long to achieve the fullness shown here. (If you submerge the boxwood in tepid water for 24 hours before making the arrangement, it should stay fresh for about a week.)

To finish, add grapes, holly berries, and spruce cones along the sides and between the larger fruits. Green chinaberries (which haven't been hit by frost) and yellow ones (which have) provide a transition in scale from the smaller holly berries to the larger grapes. Cotton bolls with the cotton removed supply starry shapes that contrast pleasingly with the round fruits.

On a smaller scale, fruit and boxwood can be combined for a more vertical emphasis *(left)*. The arrangement is made on a pyramid of wooden circles of graduated sizes, with finishing nails hammered in at regular intervals. To give the centerpiece more height, it has been placed in a brass tureen. After securing the pears, apples, and lemons on the nails and wedging the pineapple in place, tuck in boxwood and nandina berries to cover the wooden pyramid. Brass angel candleholders enclose the centerpiece and lift arrangements of boxwood and nandina berries. You can achieve a similar effect with ordinary candlesticks and a florists' tool called an epergnette, which fits into the candle cup and is packed with florists' foam.

For a more contemporary look on a buffet table (see page 56), try using lengths of fabric. Pink and green offer a variation on traditional

Christmas colors, and taffeta gives a dressy effect. Simply press the fabric and fold it in half. Then loosely knot the ends and wrap the two fabrics around each other down the length of the table. Fold under the raw edges of the ends to hide them. Crystal candlesticks, vases of pink-and-green ornamental kale, and crystal beads complete the decoration.

The tabletop *below* offers a lot to look at but is surprisingly easy to assemble. Fruit and fir branches trace a St. Andrew's cross that is anchored at the center by a miniature Christmas tree. (It's a good idea to put a piece of plastic under the branches to protect the table.) Holly, apples, kumquats, and nuts simply rest on top of the greenery. The tree is artificial, decorated with tiny candles, little wooden ornaments, and paper cones filled with nuts and cookies. You could also fill the cones with candies or mints and invite guests to help themselves. (It would be a novel way to serve dessert!)

Decorating with Natural Ornaments

Ornaments made from magnolia leaves, pine-cones, money plant, and other dried materials are easy to make and they give the tree an old-fashioned look.

To make the magnolia "flowers," collect magnolia leaves that have fallen and dried naturally. Use a hot-glue gun to glue six leaves together at the stem end, overlapping the bottoms of the leaves. Then glue three small pine-cones over this point to form the flower's center. The magnolia flowers will be too large to hang and are best displayed by resting them among the branches.

The translucent discs of money plant (also called honesty) can be assembled into a variety of shapes, including "flowers," sprays, and wreaths. You will need to build up the shapes in layers, working from the bottom up. Attach the hanger (a folded ribbon) by sandwiching it between the two bottom layers of money plant "petals." To finish the ornaments, add sumac berries, bits of juniper, hemlock cones, and white or translucent glitter.

The tiny baskets shown in the photograph are embellished with eucalyptus leaves, sumac berries, and baby's-breath. Bunches of baby's-breath are also tucked among the branches.

Garlands of popcorn and cranberries strung on thread complement the natural textures of these decorations, and miniature gingerbread cookies dusted with sugar add a homespun touch. For a Victorian feeling, burgundy velvet bows are tied to the branches and crown the tree. For a country look, you could use bows made of paper-twist ribbon.

Above right and right: Ornaments made of dried leaves, cones, and seedpods give old-fashioned charm to the tree. Assemble them with glue, ribbon, and a little glitter.

Tabletop Trees

A tabletop tree brings a touch of Christmas to any spot in the house. Use one as part of a vignette, or make several of different sizes for a miniature fantasy forest.

Three of the trees shown on these pages start with a craft foam cone. To make the hemlock-cone-and-berry tree, paint the craft foam with brown latex paint; then dip hemlock cones into low-melt hot glue and attach them to the craft foam. Finish by tucking nandina berries between the cones in a random pattern. (Don't glue them in, however. After Christmas, you can remove the berries and pack the tree away for next year.)

The starfish tree can be made with dried heather or any similar flower that has tiny blossoms and finely textured foliage all along the woody stem. Place the craft foam cone on an upside-down terra-cotta pot and, starting at the lower edge of the cone, insert stems all the way around. Push them in at an angle to create the downward sweep of the "branches." Work your way up the tree with progressively shorter stems, staggering the rows for a natural effect. Then use a hot-glue gun to attach starfish and small shells to the branches.

To begin the cinnamon-stick tree, place the craft foam cone on a heavy cardboard circle that is the diameter you want the tree to be at its base. This provides a sturdy support for the lowest layer of cinnamon sticks. (It would be a good idea to paint the cone brown, too.) Break cinnamon sticks into varying lengths; then, starting with the longest ones, dip one end into hot glue and push it into the bottom edge of the cone. Continue inserting glue-dipped cinnamon sticks into the craft foam all the way around the base to create the first row of "branches." The remaining rows of

Above left and left: A craft foam cone is the starting point for both of these trees, one made of dried flowers and sea shells, the other of hemlock cones and nandina berries.

branches are spaced further apart and staggered (see photograph). To hide the foundation, stuff bits of sphagnum moss among the cinnamon sticks. Glue a walnut to the top to serve as a finial. (If any of the cinnamon sticks seem a little wobbly, you can glue nuts between them for extra support.)

For a less conventional tabletop tree, start with a shapely branch or use a living topiary. The glittery arrangement *(above right)* is made from a gold-sprayed manzanita limb wedged in a bowl full of moist earth. The bowl is then placed in a brass container and covered with spray-painted baby's-breath. Bows, brass ornaments, and a rope of gold beads decorate the branch, which is displayed on a brass tray to strengthen its impact as a focal point.

The rosemary topiary *(above)* might ordinarily stand in the kitchen, where its leaves can be pinched off for seasoning. At Christmas, trim it with gold cherubs, tiny glass balls, and gold metallic ribbon tied in bows to create a quick coffee-table centerpiece.

Above left, above right, and right: Make a tabletop tree to suit your style. Decorate a rosemary topiary, spray a tree branch gold, or construct a cinnamon-stick tree on a craft foam cone base.

Bountiful Boxwood Boas

Evergreen garlands can bring an air of formality to any spot that will support a swag. These bounteous boas were made with armloads of boxwood, but the same garland-making technique will work with mixed greens, which can give an equally luxurious effect.

Start with a piece of clothesline the length you want the boa to be. Use spool wire, available from florists' supply shops and variety stores, to attach 3- to 4-inch-long cuttings of greenery to the clothesline. You can attach cuttings singly or in small bunches of two or three stems; lay the cuttings on the clothesline and wrap the wire around the stems and line several times (see sketch). Attach another bunch of stems on the opposite side of the clothesline in the same manner. Place a third bunch so that the foliage covers the stems of the first two bunches and, spiralling the wire around the greenery, wrap the stems and clothesline with the wire. Continue attaching cuttings, being careful to work all the way around the clothesline and to overlap the cuttings to create a full, bushy garland. The more greenery you use, the fatter the garland will be.

The boas shown here are so thick that fruit, pinecones, berries, and the popcornlike fruits of the Chinese tallow tree can be inserted with florists' picks. For extra security, the ends of the picks are dipped in hot glue before being pushed into the garland.

To hang these boxwood ropes, small eye hooks are screwed into the crown molding and the boas are attached with wire. In the foyer, one end of the boa is wired to the chain of the chandelier, where craft foam supplies the foundation for an arrangement of pepper berries, pinecones (turned so that the bottoms show), Chinese tallow tree "popcorn," and branches. Evergreen garlands should stay fresh for at least a week.

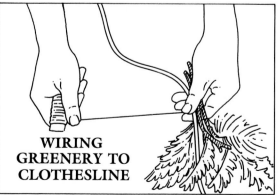

WIRING GREENERY TO CLOTHESLINE

Make the Mantel Memorable

Above: Twin arrangements of coffee fern, protea, alstroemeria, and sprayed-gold hydrangea anchor this mantel decoration, which features artificial garland embellished with fresh evergreens and dried hydrangea. For fullness along the mantel, whorls of magnolia leaves are tucked in behind the vases. Polishing them with clear acrylic floor wax will give them a high sheen.

Since a fireplace is the natural focal point of a room, the mantel is the obvious place to lavish special attention on the decorations. Symmetrical compositions are often the easiest to achieve, because you simply create a mirror image on either side of the center. But as the examples on these pages prove, symmetry need not be stiff or even especially formal.

Identical compositions frame the painting (*opposite*), but they have a loose, graceful quality because of the way the greenery spills over the edge of the mantel and the stems of the tulips arch in all directions. Craft foam covered with chicken wire provides a foundation for the juniper and fir branches. To anchor the foundation securely, it is wired to a tiny nail in the woodwork. The cranberry-filled antique hurricane lamp rests on top of the craft foam; its weight helps to balance that of the branches. The cranberries also hide the glass cylinder that holds the tulips. To create the illusion of a wreath encircling the base of the hurricane lamp, the longer branches of fir are inserted at the front and sides and shorter ones toward the rear.

For a soft line and lavish effect, try draping the mantel with fabric (*left*). Yards of gold lamé lie rumpled artfully around the flower arrangements and wind around the garland on one side of the fireplace. Lamé bows accent each corner of the mantel, and a lace tree skirt cascades over the mantel's edge.

Opposite: Branches of fir and juniper spill over the mantel's edge in these matching arrangements. Wire-edged ribbon unfurls from a cluster of apples at the center, below a hurricane lamp filled with cranberries that conceal a container of water for the tulips.

This treatment also shows how artificial garland can be used as a foundation for fresh and dried materials. Securing evergreens and gold-sprayed dried hydrangea to the artificial roping gives a much fuller and livelier effect than the roping alone would provide. And it requires less greenery than a garland of all-fresh evergreens would.

Combining fresh and everlasting materials also brings distinctive character to a rustic mantel *(below)*. Fir branches provide a bed for fresh and artificial apples, frosted-glass pinecones, and hand-carved swans and Santas. Layering a fir wreath over a vine wreath gives more depth and dimension, and red metallic

Below and left: One-of-a-kind St. Nicholases by Norma de Camp of Hendersonville, North Carolina, and hand-carved geese by Glenn Harvin of Rockwood, Tennessee, flank a fresh fir wreath layered over a vine one. At each end of the mantel, a live fir wears tiny artificial apples in celebration of the season.

hearts on foil-wrapped wire loop around the two for sparkling highlights. At each end of the mantel is a live fir that can be planted outdoors after the holidays.

If you use live trees indoors, remember that warmth can cause the trees to break dormancy; then when you plant them outside, a cold snap can kill them. If you use live trees, try to keep them inside no longer than a week to 10 days.

The appeal of artificial garland is that it is a one-time investment, and some of the synthetic materials available now are convincing substitutes for the real thing. The photograph *(at right)* shows a clever way of using such a garland, outlining a tree-shaped triangle above the mantel. Victorian-style ornaments hang along its length, and a wreath fills the apex, with a teddy bear perched inside for a whimsical focal point. A small nail or eye hook in the crown molding will hold the garland in place.

Right: Artificial garland outlines a tree shape above the mantel. It is decorated with Victorian ornaments, and a wreath fills the apex.

STITCH UP CRAZY-QUILT ORNAMENTS

The Victorian ornaments that decorate the mantel above hint at the luxurious materials and unpredictable designs of the crazy quilts that inspired them. To make some ornaments of your own, stitch together scraps of upholstery fabrics or fancy suiting and dress fabrics. Once you have pieced a fairly large square, press the seams open.

Use cookie cutters to make templates, or adapt the simple traditional shapes shown here and transfer the patterns to the pieced fabric to make the fronts. Cut the backs from a solid fabric.

Stitch assorted trims, such as tassels, sequins, beads, and lace, to the ornament fronts. Then, with right sides facing, stitch each ornament front and back together, leaving an opening for turning. Turn, stuff, and slipstitch the opening closed. Slipstitch gold trim around the edges of the ornament and tack a ribbon loop to the top for a hanger.

Presenting Potpourri with Flair

Whether you make potpourri or buy it, these aromatic mixtures can bring a delightfully Christmassy scent to a room. Because the fragrance is often elusive, potpourri is best appreciated at close quarters. Since it will be near at hand, consider making it as pretty to look at as it is pleasant to smell.

Commercially prepared potpourri becomes part of a scented centerpiece when you combine it with candles (*below left*). A bayberry candle stands in the center of a wreath of Spanish moss and eucalyptus leaves on a pewter charger. The potpourri, which includes gilded wood chips, wood shavings, and bits of dried flowers, fills in around it. A little clay bird adds a finishing touch.

You can also combine potpourri with fruit and greenery. Pomegranates, pinecones, and fresh juniper, for example, have been added to potpourri that is displayed in an old tin mold (*below right*). The result is a dried arrangement enlivened with Christmas greens and the added dimension of scent. Berries and dried flowers could also be added for more color and texture.

Finding imaginative presentations for potpourri is simply a matter of assembling objects you already have and combining them in new ways. Just remember to put the potpourri in wide bowls or shallow plates rather than tall, narrow containers so that you expose as much of the fragrant mix to the air as possible.

66

Glorious Gilded Fruit

In the 1800s, German-American families gilded nuts and apples to decorate their Christmas trees. Gilding is still a wonderful way to bring rich warmth to decorations, but we've extended the idea beyond nuts and apples to include all kinds of fresh fruits, as well as pinecones, sweetgum balls, and evergreens. It's surprisingly easy and inexpensive to do, and the results are so elegant that just a few gilded fruits can turn an ordinary arrangement of greenery into a stunning centerpiece.

Gilding works best on very firm fruit such as oranges and lemons and on underripe apples, pears, plums, and nectarines. Grapes also gild nicely. While gilded effects can be achieved with ordinary spray paint (see page 5), florists' paint, or gilt cream (see page 70), gilding powder is used here because it gives a richer look. Sold in art supply stores as bronzing powder or silk screen lining, it consists of tiny gold flakes that catch the light, creating a more shimmering quality than the other methods.

Work in a well-ventilated area and spread newspapers over the work surface. Dip fruit and other items to be gilded into clear acrylic floor wax. Be sure to coat the fruit thoroughly, because the wax serves to seal the skin so that the fruit lasts longer. Place each piece of fruit on a sheet of heavy plastic to dry and turn it occasionally to prevent a puddle of wax from forming around the bottom.

Fruit will last longer if you give it two to three coats of wax, letting it dry thoroughly between coats. If you wish, you can speed up the drying process with a hair dryer. When the final coat is completely dry, dust the fruit with gilding powder, using a cotton ball. This will leave a thin veil of gold on the skin. For an opaque, bright-gold surface, dip the cotton into the floor wax and dab it lightly over the fruit to dampen it before applying the powder. Gilding the fruit while the wax is still tacky can yield translucent effects, with just a hint of the fruit's color showing through.

Gilded grapes, plums, and pears will last about five days. Apples, oranges, and foliage

Above: Pears, pomegranates, champagne and green grapes, and holly shimmer with a veil of gold dust. Lemons, nuts, and apples have been more heavily gilded for a solid-gold look.

may last two to three weeks. For a special party, try cutting the fruit in half or quarters and gilding the cut surfaces. The cross-sections of lemons and pears have particularly interesting shapes and textures that will add variety to an arrangement of fruit.

The Scent of Citrus

A whiff of pine immediately evokes the excitement and anticipation that come with Christmas. Citrus, cinnamon, and cloves can have the same effect, instantly putting you in a holiday mood.

Fill your house with the scent of citrus this year with these artfully carved oranges, a variation on pomanders. To make these, we used a linoleum-cutting tool like the kind artists use to make block prints, but you could also use a stripper, available from kitchen shops.

To work with the artists' tool, you push into the rind; with the stripper, you pull the tool toward you. In either case, cut just to the white membrane of the orange, being careful not to pierce through it, so that juice won't leak from the fruit. Thicker-skinned oranges will work better than thin-skinned ones. Cut the rind away in spirals, chevrons, zigzags, or serpentine shapes—use the designs shown here to inspire you. (Add the peelings to stove top potpourri, or dry them to add color to dry potpourri mixes.) Make the same designs with cloves pushed into the oranges to create a different textural effect and add spice to the clean scent of citrus.

Above: Fill a room with the Christmassy aroma of clove-studded and carved oranges.

Right: You can cut designs in the rind of the orange with an artist's linoleum cutter and a U-shaped blade (called a gouge).

Christmas
Bazaar

Stenciling Adds Style To Cards and Candles

The simple technique of stenciling turns ordinary candles into unique accessories and plain stationery into handcrafted Christmas cards. To make the cards and candles shown here, as well as those on the cover, you will need stationery with matching envelopes, heavy construction paper, a craft knife, gold gilt cream, pillar candles (3″ diameter), ¼″-wide masking tape, clear acrylic spray, and gold enamel spray.

Fold the stationery in half to form a card; then unfold and lay flat. To deckle the front edge of the card, place a ruler ¼″ to ½″ from 1 of the edges parallel to the fold. Wet the edge of the card. With the ruler still in place, carefully pull away the wet paper edge.

Next, transfer the stencil patterns on page 150 to the construction paper and cut out. Position the stencil on the card front and hold firmly in place. Rub gilt cream over the openings with your fingers. Mix and match stencils as desired, but avoid smearing the design when moving the stencil. For the candle, tape the stencil in place before applying the gilt cream.

When you've finished stenciling the design, remove the stencil and spray the card or candle lightly with clear acrylic spray to prevent smudging, and allow to dry.

To make the striped candle (see cover), apply strips of ¼″-wide masking tape ¼″ apart. Spray the candle with gold enamel spray. Remove the tape when the paint is almost dry.

Above left: The versatility of stenciling lies not only in repeating the motifs on a variety of objects, but also in reversing the technique by rubbing gilt cream around the shapes you cut away from the stencils, to create still more designs.

Above: Ribbon (bottom), floss (top left), stretch lace (center), and regular floss combined with metallic floss (right) give each balloon ball a different but interesting texture.

Balloon Balls to Make with a Pop!

Who would guess these delicate ornaments are made with an old summer-camp craft technique? You may remember wrapping glue-coated string around a balloon, letting it dry, and then popping the balloon to leave an airy sphere. That same process is used here, but with metallic threads, ribbons, and embroidery floss. Remember to pop the balloon before the threads are completely dry, or the balloon, as it shrinks, will pull the ball out of shape.

Materials (for 1 ball):
small round balloon
clear-drying craft glue
water
small bowl
3 yards of regular or metallic embroidery floss or ⅛"-wide ribbon, or 12" piece of stretch lace (see Resources, page 155)
hairdryer (optional)
scraps of ribbon and floss
hot-glue gun and glue sticks
small rubber band

Blow up balloon until it is 2" to 4" in diameter.

Mix 3 parts glue with 1 part water in small bowl. Dip floss or ⅛"-wide ribbon into glue mixture, stripping out excess with fingers. Referring to photograph, wrap floss or ribbon around balloon until a secure webbing is formed.

If desired, shorten the drying process by using a hairdryer. When ball is almost dry, use a straight pin to pop balloon. Using tweezers, carefully remove balloon from inside of ball.

Tie a 12" piece of scrap ribbon in a bow and attach to top of ball with glue gun.

For hanger, loop 6" of ribbon or floss through top of ball and knot ends.

To make stretch lace ball, dip lace into glue mixture; then stretch tightly around balloon, securing ends at top of ball with rubber band. When ball is almost dry, pop and remove balloon as above.

Tie a 12" piece of scrap ribbon in a bow around secured lace at top of ball, over rubber band; then trim lace close to top so that bow hides gathered lace.

Add hanger as above.

Dress the Table in Festive Color

The traditional flying geese patchwork pattern becomes a Christmassy pine tree design when it's worked up in red and green. A striking table trimming, it can be used alone or layered over another cloth. Matching napkins with appliquéd trees complete this ensemble.

TABLE RUNNER

Materials:
patterns on page 145
¾ yard (45″-wide) red cotton
⅜ yard (45″-wide) green cotton
1 yard (45″-wide) muslin
12″ x 43″ piece of thin quilt batting
cream quilting thread
2¾ yards (½″-wide) red double-fold bias tape
threads to match fabrics

Number to Cut (4 templates):
A—24 red, 30 muslin
B—27 green
C—9 green
D—8 red, 10 muslin

Finished Size: 10″ x 40½″.

Note: Prewash fabrics, dry, and press. All seams are ¼″.

Cut pieces A-D as indicated. Following Diagram and photograph for color placement, join pieces A-D, using red As and Ds for background. Repeat to make 4 red A-D groups.

Make 5 (A-D) groups, using muslin As and Ds for background. Following photograph for placement, join the A-D groups, alternating red and muslin backgrounds.

For backing, cut a piece of muslin the same size as runner top. Stack backing (right side down), batting, and top (right side up). Baste. Following Diagram, quilt table runner, stitching ⅜″ inside seam lines.

Trim excess batting from edge of runner. Bind edges with double-fold bias tape.

NAPKINS

Materials (for 4 napkins):
pattern on page 145
1 yard (45″-wide) muslin
scraps of green cotton
green embroidery floss to match fabric
6¾ yards (½″-wide) red double-fold bias tape
threads to match fabrics

Number to Cut (1 template):
E—12 green

Note: Prewash fabrics, dry, and press. All seams are ¼″.

Cut 4 (14½″) squares of muslin. Referring to photograph for placement, center and baste 1 triangle 2½″ from 1 corner of 1 muslin square. Center and baste 2 more triangles above bottom triangle and machine-appliqué, using narrow satin-stitch.

Using 3 strands of embroidery floss, make tree trunk with very narrow satin stitches, narrowing stitches to a point at the bottom. (Top of trunk should be approximately ⅛″ wide.) Finished length of trunk should be 1″.

Bind edges with double-fold bias tape. Repeat to make 3 more napkins.

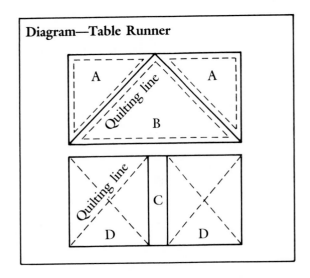

Diagram—Table Runner

Etched Snowflakes Are Easy and Elegant

Holiday china makes every meal more festive. And your guests will be impressed when you set the table with Christmas dinnerware you've made yourself. The simple art of etching turns inexpensive glass plates into elegant tableware with a dishwasher-safe finish. As with other chemicals, follow manufacturer's instructions when working with etching cream.

Materials:
pattern on page 141
clear glass plate with 7″-diameter flat
  surface
vinegar
grease pencil
peel-and-stick vinyl shelf covering
craft knife
spoon
cotton swab
etching cream

Wash plate with vinegar and warm water, keeping fingerprints off glass. Allow to dry thoroughly. Mark center on top of plate with grease pencil.

Transfer stencil to shelf covering and, on hard surface, cut out white areas with craft knife. Carefully peel off backing of shelf covering and, referring to photograph, center stencil on *bottom* of plate. Smooth stencil from center out with the back of a spoon to ensure a clean edge. Set aside for 1-2 hours to allow stencil to adhere firmly.

With a cotton swab, carefully paint etching cream over entire cutout area of stencil. Then apply a ¼″ border around edge of stencil. Make sure all cutout areas within the stencil remain covered with etching cream. Leave cream on 5-10 minutes, redistributing cream as necessary to keep all exposed glass covered. Quickly wash off etching cream with warm running water. Remove stencil and wash plate.

A Nativity In the Round

A charming holiday centerpiece, this Nativity in the Round can serve as the starting point for a variety of arrangements. Place a poinsettia in the center or mound fresh apples, oranges, and lemons on top of greenery tucked among the figures. Candlesticks of all sizes could also fill the center for a glowing decoration.

The simple shapes of the Nativity figures and the base are easy to cut. Then just use the brown marker as a quick way to outline the figures and draw the details. Or, if you prefer, use a fine-tipped woodburning pen.

Materials:
patterns on pages 142-43
graphite paper
18″ piece of 1 x 12 pine shelving
band saw or jigsaw
sandpaper
16″-diameter (¾″-thick) pine shelving circle for base
brown permanent marker
clear acrylic finish
paintbrush
18 (1½″) #6 wood screws
4 (1″) wooden ball feet
hot-glue gun and glue sticks

Using graphite paper, transfer patterns for figures to pine shelving and cut out with band saw or jigsaw. Sand sides and edges of figures and circular base smooth. Using graphite paper, transfer details of each figure onto both sides of wood. Outline figures and draw details with brown permanent marker.

Using a pencil, lightly draw a circle on top of base, ¾″ from edge. With brown permanent marker, repeat border design along penciled circle, using photograph as a guide. Gently erase pencil lines. Using paintbrush, apply acrylic finish to both sides of each figure and base and allow to dry.

For screw placement, lightly draw a circle on top and bottom of base, 1¾″ from edge. Referring to photograph for placement, center figures on circle. Attach figures to base from underneath, using 2 wood screws per figure. Gently erase pencil lines.

Divide bottom of base into fourths and mark with pencil, ¾″ from edge. At each mark, attach 1 wooden ball foot using hot-glue gun.

Border Design

Welcome the Season in Needlepoint

White yarn against a natural canvas background gives a filigreed look to needlepoint. The wall hanging, stockings, and ornaments stitch up quickly because the canvas background is left unworked and the edges are finished with bias tape or piping. Two simple border designs, one of Christmas trees and one of hearts, can be used in an alternating pattern; or each can be used alone and repeated as often as needed.

WHITE CHRISTMAS WELCOME

Materials:
charts on page 146
23¾" x 35" piece of ivory #7 mesh canvas
4 yards (½"-wide) white bias tape
4-ply white acrylic yarn
#18 tapestry needle
2 small plastic curtain rings

To bind edges of canvas, zigzag-stitch bias tape in place, mitering corners. Referring to tree border chart and using all 4 plies of yarn, work border design across 1 end of canvas, starting and ending all stitches 1 square from edge of bias tape. Work partial designs as needed to fill canvas. Turn canvas so that design is at left and work tree border design across top edge of canvas. Turn canvas again and work tree border design across right side, then bottom edge of canvas.

Referring to photograph, work "Welcome" design across center of canvas, according to chart. Skip 2 threads between pattern repeats and end stitching 1 thread from border. Using photograph as a guide, skip 4 threads above and below center "Welcome" design and work remaining lines, repeating to fill canvas and stitching partial designs as needed.

Block needlepoint. For hangers, tack plastic curtain rings to top corners on back of wall hanging.

WHITE CHRISTMAS STOCKING

Materials (for 1 stocking):
pattern and charts on pages 146-47
masking tape
11½" x 18½" piece of ivory #7 mesh canvas
4-ply white acrylic yarn
#18 tapestry needle
⅔ yard (45"-wide) white cotton for back and lining
2 yards of white piping

Note: All seams are ½".
Cover edges of canvas with masking tape to prevent unraveling. Transfer stocking pattern to canvas. Referring to heart and tree border charts and using all 4 plies of yarn, work alternating designs from top edge of stocking to bottom within traced lines, working partial designs at side and bottom edges as needed to fill canvas. Omit tent stitches and cross-stitches at the bottom of each design (see chart).

Remove tape, block needlepoint, and allow to dry thoroughly. Cut out stocking, adding ½" seam allowance.

Make pattern from needlepoint stocking. Transfer to fabric and cut 2 for lining. Reverse pattern and cut 1 for stocking back. With right sides facing and raw edges aligned, stitch piping around side and bottom edges of stocking front. With right sides facing and raw edges aligned, stitch stocking front to back on stitching line of piping, leaving top open. Turn.

To make hanger, remove cording from 6" of piping, turn raw edges to inside, and stitch along long edge. Fold hanger in half. With raw edges aligned, baste loop to right side of stocking back near left seam.

With right sides facing and raw edges aligned, stitch lining pieces together along side and bottom edges, leaving a 3" opening in seam above heel. Clip curves. Do not turn. With right sides facing, slip needlepoint stocking into lining and stitch around top of stocking, catching ends of hanger loop in seam. Turn stocking through opening in lining; then slipstitch opening closed. Tuck lining inside stocking.

WHITE CHRISTMAS ORNAMENT

Materials (for 1 ornament):
charts on page 146
6" square of ivory #7 mesh canvas
4-ply white acrylic yarn
#18 tapestry needle

Using all 4 plies of yarn, center either tree or heart border design on canvas and stitch according to chart. Repeat motif 3 times.

Referring to photograph, trim canvas 3 squares from edges of design and trim corners diagonally. Work 1 row of tent stitches around edges of design.

To make hanger, fold a 7" piece of yarn in half, thread through top of ornament, and knot ends.

A Crocheted Swag With Old-Fashioned Charm

This crocheted swag can add a Victorian look or even a country touch to your Christmas decorations. What's more, it's pretty enough to leave up year round. Stretch it along the edge of a shelf on the dining room hutch, as shown in the photograph, or use your creative flair and drape it across your mantel, catching it on the sides and at various points between with colorful ribbons or greenery. The design is based on an 8½"-long scallop, so you can make the swag as long as you like, simply by adding more scallops.

The ribbon laced through the top of the swag also gives you decorating options. Use vivid primary red, kelly green, or even a Christmas plaid to give the swag a holiday look; then after the holidays, change the ribbon color to match your interior or to reflect other seasonal events throughout the year.

Materials:
2 (282-yd.) balls of size-10 crochet cotton, ivory
#7 steel crochet hook, or size to obtain gauge
2 yards (¾"-wide) cranberry grosgrain ribbon

Gauge: 1 beading row (shell, ch 8, shell) = 2", 1 scallop (rows 1-19) = 8½".

Note: The model contains 7 (8½"-long) scallops and is approximately 60" long. Work the number of scallops needed to fit shelf.

Beading rows: Ch 16 loosely. *Row 1:* Tr in 5th ch from hook, tr in same ch, ch 1, 3 tr in same ch, ch 8, (3 tr, ch 1, 3 tr) in last st of ch-16 (shell made). Turn. *Rows 2-9:* Sl st into ch-1 sp of shell, ch 4 for first tr, (2 tr, ch 1, 3 tr) in same sp (beg shell made), ch 8, (3 tr, ch 1, 3 tr) in ch-1 sp of next shell. Turn.

Begin scallop: Row 10: Sl st to ch-sp of shell, beg shell in shell, ch 8, shell in shell, ch 7, join with a sl st to top of tr at edge of shell in row below (to form a ring). Turn. *Row 11:* Ch 4, join with a sl st to edge of next shell, (ch 1, tr in ring) 12 times, ch 1, shell in next shell, ch 8, shell in next shell. Turn. *Row 12:* Sl st to ch-sp of shell, beg shell in shell, ch 8, shell in next shell, ch 1, sk ch-1 sp, * tr in next ch-1 sp, ch 2, rep from * across, ch 1, sl st to edge of next shell on beading row. Turn. *Row 13:* Sl st to ch-2 sp, ch 6 for first tr and ch 2, tr in same sp (beg V-st made), * (2 tr, ch 1, 2 tr) in next sp, (tr, ch 2, tr) in next sp (V-st made), rep from * 4 times more, shell in shell, ch 8, shell in shell. Turn. *Row 14:* Sl st to ch-sp of shell, beg shell in shell, ch 8, shell in shell, * shell in ch-2 sp of V-st, ch 1, V-st in next ch-1 sp, ch 1, rep from * 4 times more, shell in last V-st, sl st to edge of next shell on beading row. Turn. *Row 15:* Sl st to ch-sp of shell, beg V-st in same sp, * ch 2, shell in V-st, ch 2, V-st in shell, rep from * 4 times more, shell in shell, ch 8, shell in shell. Turn. *Row 16:* Sl st to ch-sp of shell, beg shell in shell, ch 8, shell in shell, ch 2, * shell in V-st, ch 3, V-st in next shell, ch 3, rep from * 4 times more, shell in last V-st, sl st to edge of next shell on beading row. Turn. *Row 17:* Sl st to ch-sp of shell, beg V-st in same sp, * ch 4, shell in V-st, ch 4, V-st in shell, rep from * 4 times more, ch 1, shell in shell, ch 8, shell in shell. Turn. *Row 18:* Sl st to ch-sp of shell, beg shell in shell, ch 8, shell in shell, ch 1, * shell in V-st, ch 5, shell in shell, ch 5, rep from * 4 times more, shell in last V-st, sl st to edge of next shell on beading row. Turn. *Row 19:* Sl st to ch-sp of shell, ch 4, sl st to shell on beading row, (tr, ch 1) 9 times in ch-sp of shell, * ch 1, sc in ch-5 sp, ch 1, (tr, ch 1) 10 times in ch-sp of shell, rep from * 9 times more, ch 1, shell in shell, ch 8, shell in shell. Turn.

Rep rows 2-19 for desired length. Do not fasten off after last rep of row 19. Turn.

Edging: Sl st to ch-sp of shell, shell in shell, ch 8, shell in shell, ch 1, * (sc in next ch-1 sp,

ch 2) across scallop **, sc in edge of shell on beading row, ch 3, sc in edge of next shell on beading row, ch 2, rep from * across swag, end last rep at **, sl st to edge of shell on beading row. Fasten off.

Finishing: Weave in all ends. Cut a length of ribbon 2″ longer than swag. Weave ribbon through beading spaces at top edge of swag. Fold 1″ of ribbon at each end of swag to back and tack to secure.

Standard Crochet Abbreviations:
ch—chain
tr—triple crochet
st(s)—stitch(es)
sl st—slip stitch
sp—space(s)
beg—beginning
sk—skip
rep—repeat
sc—single crochet

Knit Father Christmas into Your Stocking

The legend of Father Christmas is believed to be based on the life of Saint Nicholas, a stern but kindly bishop of the fourth century who showered unexpected gifts on his neighbors. In Victorian America, this gift-giving saint was transformed into the jolly old elf we know as Santa Claus, rosy-cheeked and white bearded, with a packed sack bearing gifts for the well-behaved—and for those who try awfully hard to be.

What better way to receive those Christmas goodies than with this knitted stocking embellished with our favorite fellow. A Scandinavian border around the top and the toe enhances the design.

Materials:
charts and color key on page 145
worsted-weight wool: 3 oz. green; 2 oz.
red; 1 oz. each white, black; scraps of
pink, blue
sizes 5 and 7 knitting needles (or size to
obtain gauge)
bobbins
stitch holder
size G crochet hook

Finished Size: Approximately 23″ long.
Gauge: 9 sts and 13 rows = 2″ in St st on larger needles.
Note: Stocking is knit from the top down. To change colors, wrap old yarn over new so that no holes occur. Since it is best not to carry yarn over more than 2 stitches, it may be easier to wind yarn on bobbins while working charts.
Stocking: With smaller needles and red, cast on 66 sts. *Rows 1-6:* Work even in St st. Cut red. *Row 7:* Join green, k 1, * yo, k 2 tog, rep from * to last st, k 1. *Rows 8-12:* Work even in St st. *Rows 13-25:* Change to larger needles

and work in St st according to chart for border. *Rows 26-30:* With green, work even in St st. *Row 31:* K 35 and beg to follow chart for Santa. *Rows 32-93:* Continue following chart as established, changing colors as indicated. *Rows 94-99:* With green, work even in St st.

Heel: Join red and work on first 17 sts only, put rem 49 sts on holder. *Row 1:* K 17, turn. *Row 2 and following even-numbered rows:* Sl 1, p across. *Row 3:* K 16, turn. *Row 5:* K 15, turn. *Row 7:* K 14, turn. *Row 9:* K 13, turn. *Row 11:* K 12, turn. *Row 13:* K 11, turn. *Row 15:* K 10, turn. *Row 17:* K 9, turn. *Row 19:* K 8, yf, sl 1, yb, turn. *Row 21:* K 9, yf, sl 1, yb, turn. *Row 23:* K 10, yf, sl 1, yb, turn. *Row 25:* K 11, yf, sl 1, yb, turn. *Row 27:* K 12, yf, sl 1, yb, turn. *Row 29:* K 13, yf, sl 1, yb, turn. *Row 31:* K 14, yf, sl 1, yb, turn. *Row 33:* K 15, yf, sl 1, yb, turn. *Row 35:* K 16, yf, sl 1, yb, turn. *Row 36:* Sl 1, p across. Put these sts on holder.

Sl 17 sts from other end of holder onto needle so they can be purled (center 32 sts will be instep). Join red. *Row 1* (wrong side): P 17. *Row 2 and following even-numbered rows:* Sl 1, k across. *Row 3:* P 16, turn. *Row 5:* P 15, turn. *Row 7:* P 14, turn. *Row 9:* P 13, turn. *Row 11:* P 12, turn. *Row 13:* P 11, turn. *Row 15:* P 10, turn. *Row 17:* P 9, turn. *Row 19:* P 8, yb, sl 1, yf, turn. *Row 21:* P 9, yb, sl 1, yf, turn. *Row 23:* P 10, yb, sl 1, yf, turn. *Row 25:* P 11, yb, sl 1, yf, turn. *Row 27:* P 12, yb, sl 1, yf, turn. *Row 29:* P 13, yb, sl 1, yf, turn. *Row 31:* P 14, yb, sl 1, yf, turn. *Row 33:* P 15, yb, sl 1, yf, turn. *Row 35:* P 16, yb, sl 1, yf, turn. *Row 36:* Sl 1, k 16. Cut red.

Instep: Put all 66 sts on needle, join green and k across. *Row 2:* P across. *Row 3:* K 15, ssk, k 2 tog, k 28, ssk, k 2 tog, k 15. *Row 4:* P across. *Row 5:* K 14, ssk, k 2 tog, k 26, ssk, k 2 tog, k 14 (58 sts). *Rows 6-21:* Work even in St st. *Rows 22-34:* Work in St st according to chart for border. *Rows 35 and 36:* With green, work even in St st. Cut green.

Toe: Join red. *Row 1:* K across. *Row 2 and following even-numbered rows:* P across. *Row 3:* K 13, ssk, k 2 tog, k 24, ssk, k 2 tog, k 13. *Row 5:* K 12, ssk, k 2 tog, k 22, ssk, k 2 tog, k 12. *Row 7:* K 11, ssk, k 2 tog, k 20, ssk, k 2 tog, k 11. *Row 9:* K 10, ssk, k 2 tog, k 18, ssk,

k 2 tog, k 10. *Row 11:* K 9, ssk, k 2 tog, k 16, ssk, k 2 tog, k 9. *Row 13:* K 8, ssk, k 2 tog, k 14, ssk, k 2 tog, k 8. *Row 15:* K 7, ssk, k 2 tog, k 12, ssk, k 2 tog, k 7. Graft toe sts tog. Weave in ends.

Finishing: Make a French knot with blue for Santa's eye. Fold hem at top to inside at yo row and stitch in place. Sew stocking seam.

Hanger: With crochet hook and red, chain 16 (or desired length). Work a slip stitch in 2nd chain from hook and in each chain to end. Fasten off. Fold chain in half and tack ends to stocking.

Standard Knitting Abbreviations:
st(s)—stitch(es)
St st—stockinette stitch (k 1 row, p 1 row)
k—knit
p—purl
yo—yarn over
tog—together
rep—repeat
beg—begin(ning)
rem—remaining
sl—slip
yf—yarn forward
yb—yarn back
ssk—slip, slip, knit (sl each st k-wise, k both sts tog through back loops)

Paint a Skirt for Your Tree

Here's a tree skirt the whole family can help make—and if grandparents, aunts, uncles, or old friends come to your house every Christmas, let them join in, too. On each panel of outrigger, have one family member make a handprint and write his name next to it with shiny fabric paint. Then every year, write the date on each panel and let the person whose name appears there add one special wish. Children might want to draw a picture of the present they most hope Santa will bring—a bicycle, perhaps, or a dollhouse. Or you can simply write the words that best express your Christmas wish or the blessing you're most grateful for this season. Over the years, this tree skirt will become a scrapbook of memories for everyone to enjoy.

Materials:
patterns on pages 152-53
4¾ yards (60″-wide) ivory outrigger
2 yards (45″-wide) plaid taffeta
shiny fabric paints: red, green
acrylic paints: red, green
paintbrush
gold glitter fabric paint
threads to match fabrics
3 hooks and eyes

Note: All seams are ½″.

Enlarge patterns. Transfer panel pattern to outrigger and cut 6. Transfer side border pattern to taffeta and cut 7. Transfer bottom border pattern to taffeta and cut 6. (*Note:* Position pattern pieces on taffeta as indicated on patterns to match plaid.)

Opposite: For a unique finishing touch, spread a personalized skirt under your tree. (Instructions for the paper snowflakes are on page 84.)

Using shiny fabric paints, center and write 1 name on each panel, 1″ from bottom border. Let dry. Paint a smooth layer of acrylic paint on 1 palm of each person and press palm onto appropriate panel. Finish painting each panel by using shiny fabric paints to write wish lists or names of special gifts received on panels. Use gold glitter paint to add accent dots around names and gifts as desired. Allow to dry completely.

With right sides facing and raw edges aligned, stitch 1 side border to the right edge of 1 panel. With right sides facing and raw edges aligned, stitch 1 panel to the right edge of the side border. Continue alternating remaining side borders and panels to make a circle. Stitch the last side border to the left edge of the first panel. Do not join the final side borders together. (This will leave an opening to fit around tree.) Press seams open.

With right sides facing and raw edges aligned, stitch ends of 2 bottom border pieces together. Repeat to join remaining pieces to make 1 long strip. With right sides facing and raw edges aligned, stitch completed bottom border to bottom of tree skirt. Clip curves and press seam open. Trim ends of side borders even with edges of skirt at opening.

For backing, cut 2 (60″) lengths from outrigger. With right sides facing and raw edges aligned, stitch 60″ pieces together along 1 edge. Open fabric and press seam open. Using skirt top as a pattern and aligning skirt opening with backing seam, trace around top. Cut out backing. Remove stitching along 1 seam of backing to make opening. Press seam allowances open.

With right sides facing and raw edges aligned, stitch backing to skirt top around bottom and side borders, leaving center circle open. Clip seam allowance, turn, and press.

Turn under edges of center circle and topstitch close to edges. Overlap straight edges and sew hooks and eyes along edges to close.

Perforated Paper Snowflakes Combine Beads and Paper

The familiar cross-stitch techniques used to make these unusual ornaments take on a new look when applied to perforated paper and finished with beadwork. Because these perforated paper snowflakes are easy to assemble and inexpensive to make, you can make them in multiples for gifts or as additions to your own collection.

The durability of perforated paper makes it just as easy to work with as Aida cloth. Simply stitch the motifs onto the paper, add the beads, and hang the ornaments on your tree or in a window to admire through the holidays.

Materials (for 3 ornaments):
pattern, charts, and color key on page 140
#24 tapestry needle
embroidery floss (see color key)
Balger blending filament: red, green, white
3 (8¼″) squares of 14-count perforated paper: 1 each white, red, green
#10 crewel needle
quilting thread
glass seed beads: 1 package each red, gold, green
6 (3⅝″) squares of gold 14-count perforated paper
#8 gold metallic braid

Thread tapestry needle with 3 strands of embroidery floss and 1 strand of blending filament. Referring to chart, locate center of white 8¼″ paper square and cross-stitch design. Do not carry thread over unstitched areas.

Using crewel needle and quilting thread, attach beads as indicated on chart with half-cross stitches. Work horizontal rows from left to right or from right to left, making sure all half-crosses slant in the same direction. Work vertical and diagonal rows from top to bottom. Begin and end threads by weaving securely through stitching on back. Trim square to measure 2¼″. Repeat for red and green paper squares.

Transfer snowflake pattern to gold perforated squares and cut out.

Center 1 stitched square on 1 snowflake. Using an 18″ length of gold metallic braid, attach stitched square to snowflake by working running stitches in outer row of holes of square.

With wrong sides facing and edges aligned, stack 1 ornament front on 1 plain snowflake. Beginning at 1 corner of ornament and leaving a 4″ tail at beginning and end, work running stitches in outer row of holes, using a 36″ length of gold metallic braid. For hanger loop, knot braid tails at top of ornament and then knot ends together. Repeat for each ornament.

Stitch a Prancing Reindeer

Made from scraps of calico and felt, this sprightly reindeer requires only basic sewing skills. Allow him to prance in the center of a wreath, or hang him on your tree.

Materials:
patterns and diagram on page 149
⅛ yard (45″-wide) tan calico
scrap of brown felt
stuffing
carpet thread
4 (⅜″) buttons
threads to match fabrics
double-sided fusible web
2 black seed beads
12″ (⅛″-wide) red-and-green ribbon
2 tiny jingle bells
4″ (⅛″-wide) red ribbon

Note: All seams are ¼″.

Transfer body, foreleg, and hind leg patterns and markings to calico and cut out. Transfer pattern for antlers to felt and cut out.

With right sides facing and raw edges aligned, stitch body pieces together, leaving an opening as indicated on pattern. Clip curves and corners and turn. Stuff firmly. Slipstitch opening closed. Complete hind legs and forelegs in same manner.

To attach legs to body, use a 20″ length of doubled carpet thread and push needle from inside of leg through dot to outside of leg. Thread a button onto needle, position leg according to Diagram, and insert needle through button, back into leg, and straight through body. Refer to Diagram and attach other leg in same manner. Return needle through body.

Pull thread tightly, indenting body slightly. Knot thread on side of body to secure. Repeat for other set of legs.

Lay antlers flat on top of reindeer's head with prongs facing forward. Tack antlers tightly to head at tack line to make them stand up. Do not cut thread.

To make ears, with wrong sides facing and following manufacturer's instructions, fuse 2 (2″) squares of calico together with double-sided web. Transfer pattern to fabric and cut out. Using needle and thread from antlers, bring needle through head to ear placement line. Fold 1 ear in half and tack straight edge to head. Bring needle through head to other ear position and attach other ear in same manner.

Using same thread, bring needle out at 1 eye position and sew on bead. Stitch through head and attach bead on opposite side in same manner. Knot thread, stitch through fabric, and pull through closest seam line.

Tie ribbon in a bow around neck. Tack bells to bow, adding smaller red bow at top of bells.

For hanger, thread needle with a 7″ length of carpet thread and stitch through top of reindeer's back. Knot ends to form a loop.

Quilt a Tree of Hearts

Accented with cheery red bows, a variety of printed hearts against a quilted background will add warmth to any holiday setting.

Materials:
pattern on page 141
19½″ x 21½″ piece of off-white cotton for background
¼ yard of brown cotton for tree
scraps of green cotton prints for 18 hearts
1 yard (45″-wide) green cotton print for border and binding
24½″ x 26½″ piece of cotton for backing
24½″ x 26½″ piece of thin batting
white quilting thread
3 yards (¼″-wide) red ribbon
threads to match fabrics and ribbon
2 plastic curtain rings for hangers

Note: All seams are ¼″.

Fold background fabric in half lengthwise and press to mark vertical center.

For tree, cut strips from brown cotton in the following sizes: 1 (1⅛″ x 17″) strip for tree trunk; 1 (1⅛″ x 6″) strip, 2 (1⅛″ x 10½″) strips, and 1 (1⅛″ x 13½″) strip for branches; and 1 (1¼″ x 4¼″) strip for base.

Referring to Diagram for placement and turning edges under ⅛″, appliqué trunk down center fold of background fabric. Add branches and base.

From brown cotton, cut 8 (¾″-diameter) circles. Clip curves and turn edges of circles under ⅛″. Referring to photograph, appliqué circles over ends of branches.

Transfer heart pattern to green cotton print scraps and cut 18. Clip curves and corners and turn edges of hearts under ⅛″. Referring to photograph, place 17 hearts ¼″ below tree branches and 1 heart at top of tree. Appliqué hearts in place.

For borders, cut 2 (3″ x 21½″) strips from green cotton print for sides and 2 (3″ x 25½″) strips for top and bottom. With right sides facing and raw edges aligned, stitch a 21½″ strip to each side of wall hanging; then stitch a 25½″ strip to top and bottom edges in same manner. Press seams toward border.

Stack backing (right side down), batting, and top (right side up). Baste.

Outline-quilt around appliquéd pieces and inside green border seam on background with white thread. Referring to photograph, quilt the background fabric with a 1½″ diamond grid. Baste outside edges of border ¼″ from raw edge.

From green cotton print, cut 1½″-wide bias strips, piecing as needed to equal 3 yards. Cut into 2 (28½″) and 2 (25½″) lengths. With right sides facing and raw edges aligned, stitch bias strips to sides of wall hanging front, then to top and bottom. Fold bias to back of wall hanging, turn raw edges under, and bind.

From ribbon, cut 18 (6″) lengths and tie into small bows. Tack to top of each heart.

For hangers, tack plastic curtain rings to top corners on back of wall hanging.

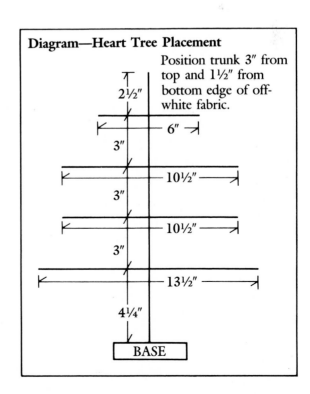

Diagram—Heart Tree Placement

Position trunk 3″ from top and 1½″ from bottom edge of off-white fabric.

2½″

6″

3″

10½″

3″

10½″

3″

13½″

4¼″

BASE

Say Hello to A Mischievous Moose

Propped in the entrance to greet your guests or sitting under the tree to keep an eye on the gifts, this clever moose is sure to start conversations. Make him from children's clothing that you buy especially for this project, or recycle holiday clothes your own children have outgrown. Either way, he will bring personality to your Christmas decorating.

Materials:
men's tan ribbed crew sock
pair of women's red knee socks
pair of child's mittens
pair of men's brown cotton work gloves
stuffing
scrap of black felt
2 (1⅛″) black shank buttons
child's long-sleeve red turtleneck (size 18 months)
child's red and green print overalls (size 18 months)
threads to match fabrics

Firmly stuff tan sock, red socks, mittens, and gloves. Make a knot in top of tan sock to hold in stuffing.

To shape head from tan sock, refer to Diagram and stitch points A to points B at neck to make a tuck that pulls head horizontal. Slipstitch securely between points.

For nose, cut a 2½″ circle from black felt. Turn edges under ¼″ and, referring to photograph, slipstitch to toe of tan sock.

For mouth, make a 1″ horizontal stitch 1½″ beneath tip of nose, pulling stitch slightly to pucker mouth.

Referring to photograph, sew 1 button to each side of tan sock for eyes. For antlers, turn ribbing of glove under and, with palm facing up, slipstitch to 1 side of tan sock 2½″ behind eye. Repeat for remaining glove.

For body, position end of tan sock inside collar of shirt. Slipstitch top edge of shirt collar around neck 1″ below tuck. Slipstitch wrist edge of 1 mitten to inside seam of each sleeve cuff. From bottom of shirt, stuff arms and upper body firmly.

For legs, stitch red socks to each other ½″ from top edges. Slide socks into overalls, positioning toes of socks about 8″ below bottom edge of overalls legs. Tack pant legs to ankles. Firmly stuff lower body.

Fit head and upper body into overalls top. Fasten overalls over shoulders.

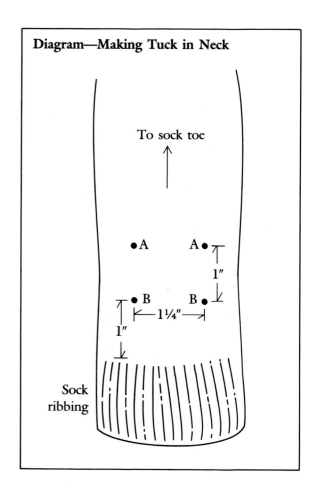

Diagram—Making Tuck in Neck

Package Toppers That Stretch to Fit

These cute package toppers do double duty as whimsical gifts and quick decorations. Stretch them around packages or tins this year, and next year the lucky recipient can use them to dress up pillows or potted plants. The felt ornaments can also be used alone. Hang them from the tree or use them to decorate the tops of packages.

To make these easy embellishments, you will need ½"-wide elastic; scraps of bright cotton prints; red, yellow, white, pink, and blue felt; stuffing; and matching threads, plus black.

To make the stretchable casing, cut a piece of elastic 1" shorter than the circumference of the item to be wrapped. From the fabric scraps, cut a 4"-wide strip 2½ times the length of the elastic. With right sides facing and raw edges aligned, fold the strip in half lengthwise. Stitch a ½" seam along the long raw edge to form a casing. Turn and press. Using a safety pin, pull the elastic through the casing; then stitch the ends of the elastic together. Fold under the casing ends and slipstitch together.

To make the felt ornaments, transfer the patterns and markings from page 144 to the felt as indicated on the patterns and cut out. Make running stitches along the broken lines as indicated on the patterns, using black thread for the cardinal and blue for the angel's wings. Make French knots for the cardinal's eyes. Straightstitch the angel's eyes and nose as indicated on the pattern.

Refer to the pattern and position the angel's hands, sleeves, face, and hair on her body, with her sleeves overlapping her hands and her hair overlapping her face. Secure to the body by blanket-stitching the sleeves in blue and the hair in yellow.

To complete the ornaments, with wrong sides facing and raw edges aligned, blanket-stitch ¾ of the way around the edges of the ornament. Lightly stuff the ornament and blanket-stitch closed. Blanket-stitch the cardinal using black thread, the star using white, the angel's body using royal blue, and the angel's wings using yellow. Do not stuff the angel's wings. Complete the angel by tacking the wings to her back.

Pin or tack the finished ornament to the elastic casing.

A Puzzle for Little Hands

Painted in primary colors, the basic shapes of this puzzle are easy for small fingers to grasp, and the familiar family faces that peek from underneath are an encouraging surprise for young puzzle workers.

Materials:
patterns on pages 154-55
tracing paper
graphite paper
9″ x 12″ piece of ¼″ plywood
scroll saw or jigsaw
sandpaper
tack cloth
water-base satin varnish
acrylic paints: ivory, bright yellow, kelly
    green, blue, red
paintbrushes
black permanent marker
photographs
8½″ x 11½″ piece of clear peel-and-stick
    vinyl shelf covering
clear tape
hot-glue gun and glue sticks
9″ x 12″ piece of ⅛″ hardboard

Transfer patterns to tracing paper; then use graphite paper to transfer heavy black cutting lines to plywood. Using scroll saw, cut out puzzle pieces along heavy black lines. Sand puzzle pieces and background smooth on all sides and wipe with tack cloth. Seal wood by applying 1 coat of varnish to pieces and background on all sides and allow to dry.

Apply 2 to 4 coats of ivory paint as a base coat to puzzle pieces and background, allowing to dry between coats.

Using graphite paper, transfer details to fronts of puzzle pieces and background. Referring to pattern, paint with acrylic paints and allow to dry. With marker, outline puzzle pieces and background and draw door knob. Apply a coat of varnish and allow to dry. Set pieces aside.

Cover photographs with vinyl shelf covering and position in puzzle openings. Trim photographs slightly larger than openings, if necessary. Secure photographs to back of background with tape.

Hot-glue background to hardboard.

Beaming with Seasonal Spirit, The Man in the Moon Is Santa

Show your seasonal spirit by creating this festive Santa Moon wall hanging and matching ornament. Cut and pieced from fabrics in patriotic reds and blues and prints of miniature stars, the diminutive wall hanging has all the charm of a country quilt.

The ornament is even easier to assemble. Fuse the Santa Moon design to the background; then stitch the fabric circles together.

Whipped up in little time, the set can become a handmade gift for a special friend or a quick holiday accent for your home.

92

WALL HANGING

Materials:
patterns on page 149
scraps of cotton: white, pink, red
4 (4½″) squares of navy cotton
2 (1¾″ x 8½″) strips of red plaid cotton
2 (1¾″ x 11″) strips of red plaid cotton
11″ square of matching fabric
    for backing
6″ (½″-wide) red grosgrain ribbon
threads to match fabrics

Note: Add ¼″ seam allowance to patterns. All seams are ¼″.

Transfer patterns to fabric scraps and cut out as follows: 2 beards from white, 2 faces from pink, 2 hats from red, 4 balls from white. Reverse patterns and repeat, except balls. Turn under seam allowances and appliqué pieces to navy squares in this order: beard, face, hat, ball (see photograph). With right sides facing and referring to photograph for placement, stitch squares together.

With right sides facing and raw edges aligned, stitch 8½″ strips to top and bottom edges of appliquéd piece and 11″ strips to side edges. With right sides facing and raw edges aligned, stitch top to backing fabric, leaving an opening for turning. Clip corners and turn. Slipstitch opening closed.

For hanger, cut ribbon in half. Fold each piece in half and tack ends to back of wall hanging at top corners.

ORNAMENT

Materials:
patterns on page 149
paper-backed fusible web
scraps of cotton: beige print, solid pink,
    solid red, solid white
2 (5½″-diameter) circles of navy cotton
    with small white stars
6″ square of thin batting
navy thread
tapestry needle
11″ (⅛″-wide) ivory satin ribbon

Note: All seams are ½″.

Following manufacturer's directions, fuse paper-backed fusible web to wrong side of fabric scraps. Transfer patterns to paper side of fusible web and cut out as follows: 1 beard from beige print, 1 face from pink, 1 hat from red, 2 balls from white. Reverse patterns and repeat, except balls. Following manufacturer's directions, remove paper backing and fuse appliqué pieces to navy print circles in this order: beard, face, hat, ball.

With right sides facing, raw edges aligned, and Santa appliqués matching, stack the navy circles on top of batting. Stitch around circle through all layers, leaving an opening for turning. Trim batting from seam. Clip curves and turn. Slipstitch opening closed.

For hanger, thread tapestry needle with ribbon. Run ribbon through top of ornament, about ½″ from edge, and pull ribbon ends even. Tie a knot in ribbon at top of ornament; then tie ribbon ends together.

Angels and Lambs from Oodles of Noodles

Friends and relatives will go "noodles" over these adorable angels and lambs made from a variety of macaronis—and they are as fun to make as they are cute. With minimal guidance from parents, kids will have a ball gluing macaronis to other noodles or to cardboard and then spray-painting them white.

MACARONI LAMB

Materials (for 1 lamb):
patterns on page 141
lightweight cardboard
scrap of black felt
craft glue
soup macaronis
2 small shell macaronis
gloss white acrylic spray paint
crystal glitter
gold thread

Note: Allow glue to dry completely between steps.

Transfer lamb pattern to cardboard and cut out. Transfer face and foot patterns to black felt and cut out.

Spread glue on 1 side of lamb, excluding face and feet. Sprinkle soup macaronis over entire glued area and allow to dry. When dry, shake off excess macaronis. Continue layering glue and soup macaronis until lamb appears to be covered with wool. For ear, glue 1 small shell macaroni close to lamb's face as indicated on pattern. Let dry. Turn lamb over and repeat for other side.

Spray lamb on both sides with white paint. When dry, apply a light coat of glue on top of macaronis and sprinkle with glitter. Shake off excess.

Glue felt face and feet to lamb on both sides.

To make hanger, thread needle with gold thread and push through top of lamb's back where indicated on pattern. Knot ends to form a loop.

MACARONI ANGEL

Materials (for 1 angel):
¾" wooden bead
craft glue
1 rigatoni noodle
soup macaronis
1 bow tie macaroni
2 elbow macaronis
gloss white acrylic spray paint
gold thread
gold fine-tipped permanent marker
miniature bell or sequin star (optional)

Note: Allow glue to dry completely between steps.

For head, glue wooden bead to top of rigatoni noodle. Referring to photograph, glue soup macaronis to top of bead to form hair. For wings, glue bow tie macaroni to back of angel. For arms, glue elbow macaronis to front of angel as shown in photograph. Spray completed angel with white paint.

To make hanger, thread gold thread through a soup macaroni on top of head. Knot ends to form a loop.

When completely dry, refer to photograph and draw eyes on face. Glue miniature bell or sequin between hands, if desired.

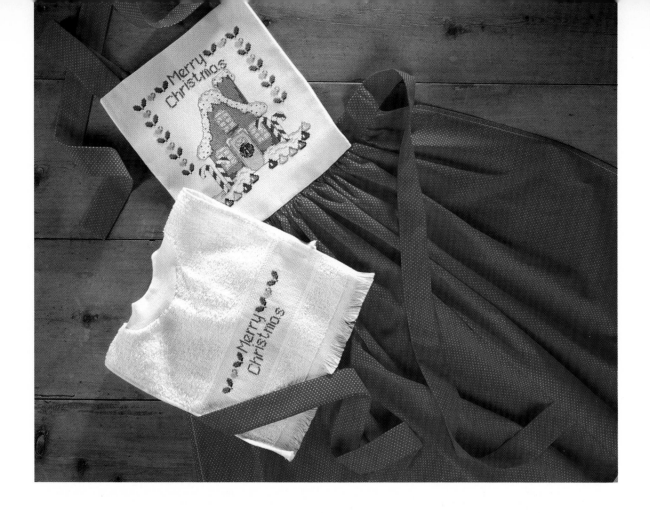

Something for Mom—and Baby, Too!

This red pindot apron, with its cross-stitched gingerbread-house bib, is a delightful accessory for a holiday hostess. The matching baby bib, edged with holly, is a simple adaptation of the apron's cross-stitch pattern applied to a purchased bib.

After stitching these quick projects, use your creativity to add a festive touch to other holiday items. You may want to convert the design for the gingerbread-house to a pillow or wall hanging. Or whip up the kitchen accompaniments shown in the photograph. For a self-lined tablecloth, with right sides facing, stack two pieces of cotton fabric a little larger than your table size, and stitch together, leaving an opening for turning. Turn and then blindstitch purchased trim to the edges, mitering the corners. For the bread cloth, stitch two rectangles of cotton fabric together, leaving an opening for turning. Turn, press, and stitch trim to

each end. Napkins can be made in the same way. The purchased kitchen towels have red and green fringe stitched near the bottom edge and again several inches higher.

BIB AND APRON

Materials:
chart and color key on page 148
purchased baby bib (parchment-
    colored with 14-count Aida insert)
embroidery floss (see color key)
#24 tapestry needle
16¼" x 17¼" piece of 14-count ivory
    Aida cloth for apron bib
1¼ yards (45"-wide) red pindot
threads to match fabrics
10¼" x 11¼" piece of ivory cotton for
    apron bib lining

For baby bib, center design on Aida insert on front of bib and work according to chart, using 2 strands of floss. The outlined portion at the top of the chart indicates the design for the baby bib. *Do not stitch the outline.*

For apron bib, center entire design on ivory Aida cloth and work according to chart. (The 16¼" edges of fabric are the top and bottom.) Use 2 strands of floss to cross-stitch and 1 strand to backstitch. Use 2 strands of crimson floss to make French knots for berries. Trim Aida cloth to 10¼" x 11¼".

Note: All seams are ⅝".

Cut the following from pindot: 1 (42" x 23") piece for apron skirt, 2 (3¾" x 30") strips for waist ties, 2 (3¾" x 27") strips for neck ties, and 1 (4¼" x 14¾") strip for waistband. Mark centers of each piece as indicated: apron skirt on 1 (42") edge, waistband on 1 (14¾") edge, and apron bib lining on 1 (10¼") edge.

For apron skirt, turn under ¼" twice along both 23" side edges and stitch a narrow hem. Repeat to hem bottom edge of skirt. At skirt top, make rows of gathering stitches ¼" and then ½" from edge.

For waist and neck ties, with right sides facing and raw edges aligned, fold each tie in half lengthwise. Stitch along long edge and 1 short end. Turn and press.

With right sides facing and raw edges aligned, baste 1 neck tie to top edge of bib lining, ⅝" in from side edge. Repeat for other neck tie at opposite corner of lining. With right sides facing and raw edges aligned, stitch cross-stitched bib front to lining along top and side edges, catching ties in seam. Trim seams and clip corners. Turn and press. Baste bottom raw edges of bib and lining together.

For waistband, with wrong sides facing, fold in half lengthwise and press. Turn unmarked long edge under ⅝" and press. Open up waistband. With right sides facing and raw edges aligned, place 1 waist tie on each end of waistband between the 2 fold lines. Baste waist ties to waistband. With right sides facing, refold waistband in half lengthwise. Stitch both ends of waistband, catching waist ties in seams. Trim seams and clip corners. Turn right side out and press.

Adjust skirt gathers to fit waistband. With right sides facing and raw edges and center marks aligned, pin bib to skirt and baste. With right sides facing and raw edges and center marks aligned, pin marked edge of waistband to skirt, with bib sandwiched between. Stitch. Trim seam and press toward waistband. Slipstitch pressed edge of waistband over seam. Press apron.

Cross-Stitch a Snowman Tote Bag

A thoughtful gift in itself, this snowman tote bag can be used during the holidays to tuck away goodies and treats. Afterwards, children can use it as a handy storage bag or carryall.

Materials:
chart and color key on page 151
12″ x 14″ piece of white 14-count Pilgrim's cloth
embroidery floss (see color key)
#24 tapestry needle
⅔ yard (45″-wide) white cotton canvas
⅔ yard (45″-wide) white cotton lining
white thread

Zigzag-stitch around raw edges of Pilgrim's cloth to prevent unraveling.

Center design on Pilgrim's cloth and work according to chart, using 3 strands of floss. Use 2 strands of red to backstitch mouth and 2 strands of black for remaining backstitches. Trim Pilgrim's cloth to 6″ x 8″.

Cut the following from cotton canvas: 1 (6″ x 8″) piece for back, 2 (3″ x 8″) pieces for sides, 1 (3″ x 6″) piece for bottom, and 2 (2½″ x 10″) strips for handles.

Cut the following from cotton lining: 2 (6″ x 8″) pieces for front and back, 2 (3″ x 8″) pieces for sides, and 1 (3″ x 6″) piece for bottom.

For handles, fold each strip in half lengthwise with right sides facing. Stitch long edges together, using ¼″ seam. Turn and press so that seam is centered on back of handle. Topstitch down both sides, ⅛″ from edges.

Note: Use ½″ seams for remainder of bag.

With right sides facing and raw edges aligned, sew canvas sides to sides of crossstitched front. Press seams open. With right sides facing and raw edges aligned, stitch bottom of bag to front and sides. Stitch back of bag to sides and bottom and turn. Turn top edge under ½″ and press. Repeat steps for lining; do not turn.

With wrong sides facing, insert lining in bag. Center and pin ½″ of each handle end between lining and bag on front and back, leaving 1″ between side seam and handle. Topstitch ⅛″ from edge around top of bag, catching handles in seam.

Celebrations
from
the Kitchen

*Recipe for Italian Cream Cake
is on page 131.*

Above: For a simple yet elegant holiday menu, try Steak and Shrimp, Noodle-Rice Casserole, Asparagus with Jalapeño Hollandaise Sauce, and Freezer Dinner Rolls.

100

Holiday Recipes to Mix and Match

A lot of thought goes into planning special holiday meals, but just about everyone has a different idea of what should be included on that perfect menu. Here we offer entrées, salads, and side dishes for you to mix and match with recipes appearing elsewhere in the chapter. Be sure to double-check the yields and make adjustments as necessary.

STEAK AND SHRIMP FOR SIX
Chutney-Cashew Spread (page 132) with Crackers
Steak and Shrimp (page 101)
Noodle-Rice Casserole (page 105)
Asparagus with Jalapeño Hollandaise Sauce
(page 104)
Freezer Dinner Rolls (page 115)
Cinnamon Tortillas with Ice Cream
(page 128)

TURKEY TENDERLOIN FOR TEN
Roasted Pepper Strips and Endive (page 132)
Turkey Tenderloins with Savory Sauce and
Dressing (page 102)
Squash-and-Snow Pea Medley (page 104)
Double Berry Salad (page 105)
Pumpkin Ice-Cream Pie (page 127)

CORNISH HENS FOR FOUR
Peppered Sesame-Cheese Twists (page 132)
Cornbread-Stuffed Cornish Hens (page 102)
Glazed Carrots and Parsnips (page 104)
Green Salad Vinaigrette (page 105)
Herb-Buttered Crescents (page 115)
Apple Cake with Caramel Sauce (page 130)

STEAK AND SHRIMP

¼ cup soy sauce
¼ cup lemon juice
2 tablespoons dry sherry
6 (1-inch-thick) beef tenderloin steaks
18 unpeeled jumbo fresh shrimp
1 clove garlic, halved
3 tablespoons butter or margarine,
   melted
   Garnish: fresh parsley sprigs
   (optional)

Combine soy sauce, lemon juice, and dry sherry in a shallow dish; add steaks, turning to coat. Cover and marinate in refrigerator 30 minutes, turning once. Remove steaks from marinade, reserving marinade.

Peel shrimp, leaving tails intact; devein and butterfly shrimp. Set aside.

Sauté garlic in butter in a large skillet over medium heat 1 minute. Add shrimp; cook just until shrimp are pink, stirring constantly. Remove shrimp from skillet. Add ⅓ cup reserved marinade to skillet; bring to a boil. Remove from heat. Return shrimp to skillet; cover to keep warm.

Place steaks on a lightly greased broiler rack. Broil 6 inches from heat 4 to 6 minutes on each side or to desired degree of doneness, brushing occasionally with reserved marinade. Arrange 3 shrimp on top of each steak, and garnish, if desired. Yield: 6 servings.

TURKEY TENDERLOINS WITH SAVORY SAUCE AND DRESSING

2½ pounds turkey tenderloins
2 tablespoons butter or margarine, melted
  Salt and pepper
¼ cup butter or margarine
¼ cup all-purpose flour
1 cup chicken broth
1 cup milk
½ teaspoon salt
¾ teaspoon pepper
¼ teaspoon poultry seasoning
  Dressing

Brush tenderloins with 2 tablespoons butter; sprinkle lightly with salt and pepper. Bake tenderloins in a lightly greased pan at 400° for 25 to 30 minutes; slice. (Interior may still be slightly pink at end of cooking.)

Melt ¼ cup butter in a heavy saucepan over low heat; add flour, stirring until smooth. Cook 1 minute, stirring constantly. Gradually add broth and milk; cook over medium heat, stirring constantly, until sauce is thickened and bubbly. Stir in ½ teaspoon salt, ¾ teaspoon pepper, and poultry seasoning.

Place Dressing on individual serving plates; serve with turkey slices and sauce. Yield: 10 servings.

Dressing:

2 (8-ounce) packages cornbread stuffing mix
6 slices whole wheat sandwich bread, crumbled
½ pound turkey sausage
1 cup chopped onion
1 cup chopped celery
2 tablespoons butter or margarine, melted
2 eggs, beaten
1½ cups milk
¾ cup chicken broth
½ teaspoon poultry seasoning
¼ teaspoon pepper

Combine stuffing mix and bread in a large bowl; set aside. Cook sausage, onion, and celery in butter in a large skillet until sausage is browned, stirring to crumble sausage. Stir into stuffing mixture. Add eggs, milk, chicken broth, poultry seasoning, and pepper, mixing ingredients well.

Spoon mixture into 10 portions on a lightly greased baking sheet. Cover and bake at 400° for 20 minutes. Uncover and bake for an additional 10 minutes. Yield: 10 servings.

CORNBREAD-STUFFED CORNISH HENS

1 (6-ounce) box cornbread stuffing mix
¾ cup water
½ cup sliced celery
1 (8-ounce) container soft cream cheese with chives and onions, divided
½ cup fresh cranberries, cut in half
¼ cup coarsely chopped pecans
4 (1- to 1½-pound) Cornish hens
  Vegetable oil
  Garnishes: fresh parsley sprigs, cranberries (optional)

Combine vegetable-seasoning packet from box of cornbread stuffing mix with water and celery in a saucepan; bring to a boil. Cover, reduce heat, and simmer 5 minutes. Stir in stuffing crumbs, ¼ cup cream cheese, cranberries, and pecans. Cover; remove from heat. Let stand 5 minutes.

Remove giblets from hens; reserve for other uses. Rinse hens with cold water, and pat dry. Gently loosen skin on breast of each Cornish hen; spread remaining cream cheese evenly under skin.

Stuff hens with cranberry mixture, and close cavities. Secure with wooden picks; truss. Place hens, breast side up, in a shallow pan, and brush with oil. Bake at 325° for 1 to 1½ hours or until juices run clear when thigh is pierced with a fork. Garnish, if desired. Yield: 4 servings.

These juicy stuffed hens are a flavorful
surprise—under the crisp brown skin is a layer of
herbed cream cheese. Complete the menu with
Glazed Carrots and Parsnips, Green Salad
Vinaigrette, and Herb-Buttered Crescents.

SQUASH-AND-SNOW PEA MEDLEY

2 cloves garlic, crushed
¼ cup butter or margarine
1 pound zucchini, cut into 2-inch strips
1 pound yellow squash, cut into 2-inch strips
¼ pound fresh snow pea pods or ½ (6-ounce) package frozen snow pea pods, thawed
½ teaspoon dried whole oregano

Place garlic and butter in a 12- x 8- x 2-inch baking dish. Microwave at HIGH 1 minute or until butter melts. Add remaining ingredients, mixing well. Cover tightly with heavy-duty plastic wrap; fold back a small corner of wrap to allow steam to escape. Microwave at HIGH 5 to 6 minutes or until the vegetables are crisp-tender, stirring after 3 minutes. Yield: 10 servings.

Above: This traditional meal is sure to be a favorite. Counterclockwise from front: Squash-and-Snow Pea Medley, Turkey Tenderloins with Savory Sauce and Dressing, Double Berry Salad.

ASPARAGUS WITH JALAPEÑO HOLLANDAISE SAUCE

1½ pounds fresh asparagus or 2 (10-ounce) packages frozen asparagus spears*
1 (0.9-ounce) package hollandaise sauce mix
2 tablespoons grated Parmesan cheese
1 tablespoon seeded and diced jalapeño pepper
2 teaspoons diced pimiento

Snap off tough ends of asparagus. Remove scales with a vegetable peeler or knife, if desired. Place asparagus in a vegetable steamer over boiling water; cover and steam 8 to 10 minutes or until crisp-tender. Arrange asparagus on a serving plate; keep warm.

Prepare hollandaise sauce mix according to package directions; stir in Parmesan cheese, jalapeño pepper, and pimiento. Serve over asparagus. Yield: 6 servings.

* 1½ pounds fresh broccoli or 2 (10-ounce) packages frozen broccoli spears may be substituted. Trim off large leaves of fresh broccoli, and remove tough ends of lower stalks. Wash thoroughly, and cut into spears. Place broccoli in a vegetable steamer over boiling water; cover and steam 8 to 10 minutes or until crisp-tender.

GLAZED CARROTS AND PARSNIPS

¾ pound carrots
¾ pound parsnips
⅔ cup chicken broth
3 tablespoons butter or margarine
1 tablespoon sugar
¼ teaspoon salt

Scrape carrots and parsnips; cut into thin diagonal slices.

Combine vegetables, chicken broth, and remaining ingredients in a large heavy skillet;

104

bring to a boil. Cover, reduce heat, and simmer 5 minutes or until vegetables are crisptender. Remove vegetables, keeping warm. Bring liquid to a boil; boil 3 minutes or until slightly thickened. Return vegetables to skillet, stirring to coat. Yield: 4 servings.

NOODLE-RICE CASSEROLE

¼ cup butter or margarine
3 ounces angel hair spaghetti, broken
    into 1½-inch pieces
1 cup long-grain rice, uncooked
¾ teaspoon chicken-flavored bouillon
    granules
2 cups water
1 (10½-ounce) can French onion soup,
    undiluted
1 teaspoon soy sauce
1 (8-ounce) can sliced water chestnuts,
    drained

Melt butter in a large skillet. Add angel hair spaghetti; cook until golden brown, stirring constantly. Remove from heat.

Stir in remaining ingredients; pour into a lightly greased 8-inch square baking dish. Bake, uncovered, at 350° for 40 to 50 minutes, stirring once. Yield: 6 servings.

GREEN SALAD VINAIGRETTE

6 cups mixed salad greens
1 small red onion, sliced
4 slices bacon, cooked and crumbled
    Roasted Pecans
¼ cup olive oil
2 tablespoons raspberry vinegar
1½ teaspoons sugar
⅛ teaspoon salt
    Dash of white pepper

Combine first 4 ingredients in a large bowl. Combine olive oil and remaining ingredients in a jar; cover tightly, and shake vigorously. Pour over salad mixture, tossing to coat. Serve immediately. Yield: 4 servings.

Roasted Pecans:

2 tablespoons sugar
1 tablespoon butter or margarine
1 tablespoon orange juice
¼ teaspoon ground cinnamon
⅛ teaspoon red pepper
1 cup pecan halves

Combine all ingredients in a large heavy skillet; cook over medium heat, stirring constantly, until sugar dissolves. Spread pecans on a lightly greased baking sheet; bake at 200° for 1 hour, stirring every 15 minutes. Let cool completely; store in an airtight container. Yield: 1 cup.

DOUBLE BERRY SALAD

1 (3-ounce) package raspberry-flavored
    gelatin
1 cup boiling water
1 (16-ounce) can whole-berry
    cranberry sauce
¾ cup finely chopped celery
½ cup chopped pecans
    Lettuce leaves

Dissolve gelatin in boiling water. Chill until mixture is the consistency of unbeaten egg white. Stir in cranberry sauce, celery, and pecans.

Spoon mixture into lightly oiled individual molds or a 4-cup mold. Cover and chill until firm. Unmold onto lettuce leaves. Yield: 10 servings.

A Luncheon for Holiday Crafters

Fellowship across the table is a long-standing tradition among Southerners of all ages. And the holiday season lends itself to a creative variety of parties. Why not bring family and friends together for a special kind of luncheon? Start with a morning of handicrafts—simple projects that everyone can make. Then serve a tasty hot meal. A craft luncheon is a delightful way to usher in the holidays while creating wonderful memories as well as charming Christmas gifts.

Cornmeal-Cheese Straws
Winter Warmer Spiced Tea
Chicken-and-Shrimp Florentine
Holiday Aspic
Sourdough Wedges
Jam Cake with Caramel Frosting or
Kahlúa-Chocolate Cake

CORNMEAL-CHEESE STRAWS

½ cup butter or margarine, softened
2 cups (8 ounces) finely shredded sharp Cheddar cheese
¼ cup water
1 cup all-purpose flour
½ cup white cornmeal
1 teaspoon paprika
½ teaspoon salt
¼ teaspoon red pepper

Beat butter and cheese at medium speed of an electric mixer until creamy. Add water, beating well. Combine flour and remaining ingredients; gradually add to cheese mixture, beating until blended.

Use a cookie press to shape dough into strips, following manufacturer's instructions.

Above: Welcome fellow crafters with Winter Warmer Spiced Tea and Cornmeal-Cheese Straws.

(If a small serrated disc is not available, place a small piece of tape over each side of the serrated disc to leave a ¾-inch opening.) Place strips on ungreased baking sheets; cut into 2-inch strips. Bake at 375° for 10 to 12 minutes or until lightly browned. Remove to wire racks to cool. Store in airtight containers, placing wax paper between layers. Yield: 10½ dozen.

WINTER WARMER SPICED TEA

10 to 12 whole cloves
2 (3-inch) sticks cinnamon
2 quarts boiling water
4 family-size tea bags
2 quarts apple juice
2½ cups pineapple juice
2½ cups orange juice
½ cup lemon juice
¼ cup sugar

Tie cloves and cinnamon sticks in a cheesecloth bag; set aside.

Pour boiling water over tea bags in a Dutch oven; cover and steep 5 minutes. Remove tea bags, squeezing gently.

Add spice bag, apple juice, and remaining ingredients to Dutch oven; bring to a boil over medium heat. Cover, reduce heat, and simmer 30 minutes. Remove spice bag, and serve hot. Yield: 5 quarts.

CHICKEN-AND-SHRIMP FLORENTINE

- 1½ pounds unpeeled medium-size fresh shrimp
- 6 chicken breast halves, skinned and boned
- ¼ teaspoon garlic powder
- ¼ teaspoon pepper
- 3 tablespoons butter or margarine
- ¾ cup dry white wine
- 3 (10-ounce) packages frozen chopped spinach
- 1 (8-ounce) package cream cheese, cubed
- 1 (3-ounce) package cream cheese, cubed
- 3 tablespoons butter or margarine
- 3 tablespoons grated Parmesan cheese
- 2 (10¾-ounce) cans cream of mushroom soup, undiluted
- 1 (10¾-ounce) can cream of celery soup, undiluted
- 1 (4-ounce) jar diced pimiento, drained
- 1 cup soft breadcrumbs
- 2 tablespoons butter or margarine, melted
- Garnishes: spinach leaves, pimiento rose (optional)

Peel and devein shrimp; set aside.

Sprinkle chicken with garlic powder and pepper, and place in a lightly greased 13- x 9- x 2-inch pan. Dot with 3 tablespoons butter, and pour wine over top. Broil 7 inches from heat 11 to 13 minutes or until lightly browned, turning once. Add shrimp; broil 5 to 8 minutes or until shrimp turn pink, stirring once. Remove from oven; cool slightly. Drain and reserve drippings. Cut chicken into bite-size pieces; set chicken and shrimp aside.

Cook spinach according to package directions, omitting salt; drain well between layers of paper towels.

Combine cream cheese and 3 tablespoons butter in a heavy saucepan; cook over medium heat, stirring constantly, until cream cheese melts. Remove from heat; stir in Parmesan cheese and spinach.

Above: The menu for the crafters' luncheon includes, clockwise from front: Chicken-and-Shrimp Florentine, Sourdough Wedges, Jam Cake with Caramel Frosting, and Holiday Aspic.

Combine reserved drippings and soups; stir well. Gently stir in spinach mixture, chicken, shrimp, and diced pimiento. Spoon into a lightly greased 13- x 9- x 2-inch baking dish. Combine breadcrumbs and butter; sprinkle on top. Bake at 350° for 40 to 45 minutes or until heated. Garnish, if desired. Yield: 12 servings.

Above: Thoughtfully handcrafted Christmas gifts can be as much fun to make as they are to give. Combining a craft workshop with a luncheon will create one of the most memorable occasions of the holidays.

HOLIDAY ASPIC

   1 (3-ounce) package lemon-flavored
      gelatin
   1 cup boiling water
   2 envelopes unflavored gelatin
2⅔ cups vegetable juice cocktail, divided
  ¾ cup white vinegar
1½ tablespoons lemon juice
  ½ to ¾ teaspoon hot sauce
   1 cup chopped celery
  ½ cup chopped green pepper
  ½ cup pimiento-stuffed olives, sliced
      Bibb lettuce leaves

Dissolve lemon-flavored gelatin in 1 cup boiling water.

Sprinkle unflavored gelatin over 1 cup vegetable juice cocktail in a saucepan; let stand 1 minute. Cook over low heat, stirring until gelatin dissolves. Add remaining vegetable juice, lemon gelatin mixture, vinegar, lemon juice, and hot sauce; chill until the consistency of unbeaten egg white. Fold in celery, green pepper, and olives; pour into a lightly oiled 6-cup mold. Cover and chill. Unmold onto lettuce leaves. Yield: 12 servings.

SOURDOUGH WEDGES

   1 (12-ounce) package sourdough rolls
  ½ cup butter or margarine, melted
2½ tablespoons grated Parmesan cheese
  ½ teaspoon paprika

Slice each roll in half horizontally; cut each piece in half. Brush cut surfaces with butter. Combine grated Parmesan cheese and paprika; sprinkle on cut surfaces. Place bread on a baking sheet, and broil 6 inches from heat 2 to 3 minutes or until golden brown. Yield: 3 dozen.

KAHLÚA-CHOCOLATE CAKE

   1 (18.25-ounce) chocolate cake mix
   1 (8-ounce) carton sour cream
   4 eggs
  ⅔ cup Kahlúa
  ¾ cup vegetable oil
   1 cup semisweet chocolate morsels
      Chocolate Frosting

Combine first 5 ingredients in a large mixing bowl. Beat at medium speed of an electric mixer 3 to 5 minutes. Stir in chocolate morsels. Spoon into a greased and floured 10-inch Bundt pan. Bake at 325° for 55 minutes or until a wooden pick inserted in center comes out clean. Cool in pan 30 minutes; remove from pan, and let cool on a wire rack. Drizzle cake with Chocolate Frosting. Yield: one 10-inch cake.

Chocolate Frosting:

    2 tablespoons butter or margarine
    2 tablespoons cocoa
    2 tablespoons Kahlúa
    2 teaspoons milk
    1 cup sifted powdered sugar
    ¼ teaspoon vanilla extract

Combine butter, cocoa, Kahlúa, and milk in a small saucepan; bring to a boil, stirring until butter melts. Stir in powdered sugar and vanilla. Yield: ½ cup.

JAM CAKE WITH CARAMEL FROSTING

    1 cup shortening
    2 cups sugar
    3 eggs
    3 cups all-purpose flour, divided
    1 teaspoon baking soda
    1 teaspoon ground cloves
    1 teaspoon ground cinnamon
    1 teaspoon ground allspice
    1 teaspoon ground nutmeg
    1 cup buttermilk
    1 (12-ounce) jar strawberry preserves
    2 cups chopped pecans
    1 cup raisins
      Caramel Frosting

Beat shortening; gradually add sugar, beating at medium speed of an electric mixer. Add eggs, one at a time; beat after each addition.

Combine 2¾ cups flour, soda, and spices; add to creamed mixture alternately with buttermilk, beginning and ending with flour mixture. Mix after each addition. Stir in strawberry preserves.

Combine pecans, raisins, and remaining ¼ cup flour; stir into batter.

Pour batter into 3 greased and floured 9-inch round cakepans. Bake at 350° for 25 to 30 minutes or until a wooden pick inserted in center comes out clean. Cool in pans 10 minutes; remove from pans, and let cool completely on wire racks.

Spread Caramel Frosting between each layer and on top and sides of the cake. Yield: one 3-layer cake.

Caramel Frosting:

    3 cups sugar, divided
    1 tablespoon all-purpose flour
    ½ teaspoon salt
    1 cup milk
    ¾ cup butter or margarine
    1 teaspoon vanilla extract

Sprinkle ½ cup sugar in a shallow heavy 3½-quart Dutch oven; cook over medium heat, stirring constantly, until sugar melts (sugar will clump) and turns light golden brown. Remove from heat.

Combine remaining 2½ cups sugar, flour, and salt in a saucepan; stir in milk. Cook mixture over medium heat until sugar dissolves, stirring constantly. Add butter, and bring to a boil.

Gradually pour one-fourth of hot mixture into caramelized sugar, stirring constantly; add remaining hot mixture. (Mixture will lump, but continue stirring until it melts.)

Return to heat; cook over medium heat, stirring occasionally, until mixture reaches 230° (about 5 minutes); stir in vanilla.

Remove from heat. Beat mixture with a wooden spoon or at medium speed of an electric mixer until frosting is of spreading consistency (about 15 minutes). Yield: enough for one 3-layer cake.

Start the Season with a Breakfast Party

School is out for the Christmas holidays, and the teens at your house are ready for fun. Before the beginning of traditional family activities, perhaps they can have a special time with their friends. A pajama party is just the way for them to kick off their holiday break.

Let the party continue in the morning when the teenagers take over the kitchen to prepare their own breakfast. These recipes are simple enough for even an inexperienced cook, and one taste of Applesauce Cream will prove that a recipe does not have to be difficult to be delicious. Teens will certainly agree that creamy Cranberry Butter slowly melting over Whipping Cream Waffles is a wonderful way to begin a day. Fresh fruit, Pineapple Breakfast Drink, and, if you wish, cups of hot chocolate round out this hearty meal.

Granola Pancakes
Whipping Cream Waffles
Cranberry Butter Applesauce Cream
Fresh fruit
Pineapple Breakfast Drink
Hot Chocolate

GRANOLA PANCAKES

   1 egg, beaten
   1 cup plus 2 tablespoons buttermilk
   1 tablespoon vegetable oil
   ½ cup all-purpose flour
   ½ cup whole wheat flour
   1½ teaspoons baking powder
   ½ teaspoon baking soda
   ⅓ cup natural granola cereal
   1 tablespoon flaked coconut (optional)
   ½ teaspoon ground cinnamon

Combine first 3 ingredients; stir well. Combine flours and remaining ingredients; stir into buttermilk mixture.

For each pancake, pour ¼ cup batter onto a hot, lightly greased griddle. Turn pancakes when tops are covered with bubbles and edges look cooked. Serve with Cranberry Butter, Applesauce Cream, syrup, or honey. Yield: 8 (4-inch) pancakes.

Above: Whipping Cream Waffles with Applesauce Cream and Granola Pancakes are a delightful way to begin a day. Add a serving of fresh fruit to create a plate that is as pretty as it is tasty.

110

WHIPPING CREAM WAFFLES

  ⅔ cup all-purpose flour
  1 teaspoon baking powder
  ⅛ teaspoon salt
  ⅓ cup sugar
  2 eggs, separated
  1 cup whipping cream, whipped
  1 tablespoon butter or margarine,
    melted

Combine first 4 ingredients. Beat egg yolks; fold in whipped cream and butter. Fold flour mixture into whipped cream mixture.

Beat egg whites at high speed of an electric mixer until stiff peaks form; fold into batter (batter will be thick). Cook in a preheated, oiled waffle iron until lightly browned. Serve with Cranberry Butter, Applesauce Cream, syrup, or honey. Yield: 2 (8-inch) waffles.

CRANBERRY BUTTER

  ½ cup butter, softened
  ¼ cup sifted powdered sugar
  2 tablespoons whole-berry cranberry
    sauce

Combine butter and sugar; beat at medium speed of an electric mixer until blended; stir in cranberry sauce. Spoon mixture into a butter crock, or shape as desired. Cover and chill. Serve with waffles or pancakes. Yield: ⅔ cup.

APPLESAUCE CREAM

  ½ cup whipping cream
  ½ cup applesauce
  ¼ cup sifted powdered sugar
  1 tablespoon lemon juice

Beat whipping cream at medium speed of an electric mixer until soft peaks form; fold in applesauce, powdered sugar, and lemon juice. Cover and chill. Serve with waffles or pancakes. Yield: 1½ cups.

Above: Bright Christmas china, place mats, and serving dishes make the setting festive. For a quick table decoration, wrap a potted amaryllis with fabric and mound Spanish moss around the bulb.

PINEAPPLE BREAKFAST DRINK

  2 (8-ounce) cans unsweetened crushed
    pineapple, undrained and chilled
  2 large ripe bananas, peeled, sliced, and
    frozen
  ½ cup water
  1 cup instant nonfat dry milk powder
  2 tablespoons sugar
  2 teaspoons lemon juice

Combine half of all ingredients in container of an electric blender; blend until smooth. Add enough ice to make mixture in blender measure 4 cups; process until smooth and thickened. Repeat procedure with remaining ingredients. Serve immediately. Yield: 2 quarts.

Beverages

CAPPUCCINO

3 cups brewed coffee
3 cups half-and-half
½ cup crème de cacao
¼ cup rum
¼ cup brandy
Sugar (optional)

Combine all ingredients in saucepan; cook over medium heat until hot. Serve immediately. Yield: 1¾ quarts.

GAELIC COFFEE

2 tablespoons Irish whiskey
¾ cup brewed hot coffee
1 to 2 teaspoons sugar
3 tablespoons whipped cream

Pour whiskey into an 8-ounce stemmed glass. Add coffee and sugar, stirring well. Top with whipped cream; serve immediately. Yield: 1 serving.

FRUIT DAIQUIRIS

1 (6-ounce) bottle maraschino cherries
1 (6-ounce) can frozen orange juice concentrate, thawed and undiluted
1 (6-ounce) can frozen pink lemonade concentrate, thawed and undiluted
7 cups water
2 cups light rum
⅓ cup lemon juice
½ (6-ounce) can frozen limeade concentrate, thawed and undiluted
1 cup sifted powdered sugar

Drain cherries, reserving juice; set cherries aside. Combine cherry juice, orange juice concentrate, and remaining ingredients; stir well,

and freeze until firm. To serve, spoon 3 to 4 cups frozen mixture at a time into container of an electric blender; blend until slushy. Keep remaining mixture frozen until needed. Garnish with cherries. Yield: 2½ quarts.

SPICY BLOODY MARY

1 (48-ounce) can tomato juice
1 (10½-ounce) can condensed beef broth, undiluted
¼ cup Worcestershire sauce
2 tablespoons lime juice
1½ teaspoons seasoned salt
1½ teaspoons celery salt
1 teaspoon instant minced onion
1 teaspoon celery seeds
½ teaspoon freshly ground pepper
3 to 4 dashes of hot sauce
1 to 2 cups vodka
Garnish: celery stalks (optional)

Combine first 10 ingredients; chill. Stir in vodka just before serving. Garnish each serving, if desired. Yield: 8 to 9 cups.

CHERRY-FRUIT PUNCH

2 cups sugar
4 (3-ounce) packages cherry-flavored gelatin
4 cups boiling water
1 (46-ounce) can pineapple juice
1 (6-ounce) can frozen orange juice concentrate, thawed and undiluted
1 (6-ounce) can frozen lemonade concentrate, thawed and undiluted
1 (1-ounce) bottle almond extract
1 gallon water

Dissolve sugar and gelatin in boiling water in a large bowl; stir in pineapple juice and remaining ingredients. Cover and freeze at least 8 hours.

Remove from freezer 2 hours before serving. Place in a punch bowl; stir until slushy. Yield: 2 gallons.

RASPBERRY COOLER

1 (10-ounce) package frozen
    raspberries, thawed and undrained
1 (6-ounce) can frozen lemonade
    concentrate, thawed and undiluted
2 cups water
3 (10-ounce) bottles lemon-lime
    carbonated beverage, chilled

Place raspberries in container of an electric blender; process until smooth. Strain mixture, discarding seeds. Combine raspberry puree, lemonade concentrate, and water; chill. Stir in carbonated beverage just before serving over ice. Yield: 1¾ quarts.

CITRUS PUNCH

1 (46-ounce) can pineapple juice
1 (46-ounce) can apple juice
1 (12-ounce) can frozen lemonade
    concentrate, thawed and undiluted
½ cup sugar
4 (33.8-ounce) bottles ginger ale,
    chilled
    Citrus Ice Ring (optional)

Combine first 4 ingredients, stirring until sugar dissolves. Divide mixture evenly into 4 heavy-duty zip-top plastic bags; seal securely. Freeze until firm.

To serve, partially thaw mixture in punch bowl as needed, adding 1 bottle ginger ale to each bag of fruit juice mixture; stir gently. Add Citrus Ice Ring, if desired. Yield: 7½ quarts.

Citrus Ice Ring:

6 cups water
Oranges, limes, lemons

Boil water 1 minute; let cool to room temperature. Pour 3 cups of the water into a 6-cup ring mold; freeze. Set remaining water aside.

For each citrus rose, cut a thin slice from bottom of fruit using a sharp paring knife; discard. Beginning at top of fruit, peel a continuous strip ½- to ¾-inch wide. Starting with first portion cut, coil strip to look like a rose, coiling tightly at first to form center, and gradually coiling more loosely to form outer petals. Secure with wooden picks.

Arrange citrus roses as desired on top of ice ring. Slowly fill mold with remaining water. (Citrus roses will float.) Partially freeze ice ring; remove wooden picks from citrus roses and return ice ring to freezer until firm.

Let mold sit at room temperature 5 minutes or until loosened. Carefully remove ice ring from mold, and float in punch.

Above: Garnish Citrus Punch with roses you make yourself from lemon, lime, and orange peels.

Above: Herb-Buttered Crescents will melt in your mouth. They're light and flaky, with butter and chives baked inside. You can make the dough ahead of time and roll up the crescents an hour before dinner.

114

Breads

HERB-BUTTERED CRESCENTS

- 1 cup milk
- ½ cup sour cream
- ½ cup butter or margarine
- ½ cup sugar
- 2 packages dry yeast
- ½ cup warm water (105° to 115°)
- 2 eggs, beaten
- 2 teaspoons salt
- 5½ to 6 cups all-purpose flour, divided
  Herb Butter

Combine first 4 ingredients in a saucepan; cook over low heat until butter melts, stirring occasionally. Cool to 105° to 115°.

Dissolve yeast in warm water in a large mixing bowl; let stand 5 minutes. Stir in milk mixture, eggs, salt, and 2 cups flour; beat at medium speed of an electric mixer 2 minutes. Stir in enough remaining flour to make a medium-stiff dough. Place in a well-greased bowl, turning to grease top. Cover and refrigerate at least 8 hours.

Turn dough out onto a floured surface, and knead 1 minute or until smooth and elastic. Divide dough into 4 portions. Roll each portion into a 12-inch circle on a lightly floured surface, and spread with 2 tablespoons Herb Butter. Cut each circle into 12 wedges; roll each wedge, jellyroll fashion, beginning at wide end. Place about 2 inches apart on greased baking sheets, point side down, curving into crescent shapes. Cover and let rise in a warm place (85°), free from drafts, 40 to 45 minutes or until doubled in bulk. Bake at 375° for 10 to 15 minutes or until rolls are golden brown. Yield: 4 dozen.

Herb Butter:

- ½ cup butter, softened
- 2 tablespoons chopped chives
- 1½ tablespoons minced fresh parsley
- 2 teaspoons lemon juice
- ⅛ teaspoon red pepper

Combine all ingredients. Yield: ½ cup.

Note: Dough for crescent rolls may be refrigerated for up to 2 days.

FREEZER DINNER ROLLS

- 2½ cups water
- 2 tablespoons molasses
- ¾ cup shortening
- 3½ to 4½ cups all-purpose flour, divided
- 1½ cups whole wheat flour, divided
- 1½ cups rye flour, divided
- 2 teaspoons salt
- 2 teaspoons caraway seeds
- 2 eggs, beaten
- ½ cup sugar
- 2 packages dry yeast

Combine water, molasses, and shortening in a small saucepan; cook over low heat until shortening melts, stirring occasionally. Cool to 120° to 130°.

Combine 2 cups all-purpose flour, ½ cup whole wheat flour, ½ cup rye flour, and remaining 5 ingredients in a large mixing bowl; stir well.

Gradually add liquid mixture to flour mixture, beating 4 minutes at medium speed of an electric mixer. Stir in remaining 1 cup whole wheat flour, 1 cup rye flour, and enough remaining all-purpose flour to make a stiff dough.

Turn dough out onto a heavily floured surface, and knead until smooth and elastic (about 5 minutes). Place in a well-greased bowl, turning to grease top. Cover and let rest 20 minutes. Punch dough down; shape into 36 balls. Place balls on a lightly greased baking sheet. Cover with plastic wrap; freeze until firm. Transfer frozen balls to heavy-duty zip-top plastic bags. Freeze up to 1 month.

Remove from freezer; place 2 inches apart on greased baking sheets. Cover and let rise in a warm place (85°), free from drafts, 1½ to 2 hours or until doubled in bulk. Bake at 375° for 15 minutes or until lightly browned. Yield: 3 dozen.

PEASANT BREAD

- 1 package dry yeast
- 2 tablespoons warm water (105° to 115°)
- ¼ teaspoon sugar
- 1 cup warm water (105° to 115°)
- 1 tablespoon grated unsweetened chocolate
- 1½ tablespoons vegetable oil
- 1½ teaspoons salt
- 1½ tablespoons molasses
- ¼ teaspoon ground cumin
- 1 cup unbleached white flour
- 1¼ cups whole wheat flour
- 1 cup rye flour
- 2½ tablespoons cornmeal
- 2½ tablespoons wheat bran
  Cornmeal
- 1 egg white
- 1 tablespoon water

Dissolve yeast in 2 tablespoons water in a large mixing bowl; stir in sugar, and let stand 5 minutes.

Add 1 cup water and next 5 ingredients to yeast mixture, mixing well. Stir in unbleached white flour; beat at low speed of an electric mixer until smooth. Gradually stir in whole wheat flour and next 3 ingredients.

Turn dough out onto a lightly floured surface, and knead until smooth and elastic (about 10 minutes). Place in a well-greased bowl, turning to grease top. Cover and let rise in a warm place (85°), free from drafts, 1 hour or until doubled in bulk. (Or, to let dough rise in the microwave, set non-metal bowl in a large round shallow dish; pour hot water to a depth of 1 inch in bottom dish. Cover dough loosely with wax paper. Microwave at MEDIUM LOW [30% power] 2 minutes; let stand in microwave 5 minutes. Repeat microwaving and standing 3 times or until dough is doubled in bulk, giving dish a quarter-turn after each microwaving period. Carefully turn dough over in bowl if dough's surface appears to be drying out. Remove from oven.)

Punch dough down, and knead on a lightly floured surface 5 minutes. Shape dough into a ball, and place in a greased 8-inch round cakepan that has been dusted with cornmeal. Cover and let rise in a warm place, free from drafts, 35 minutes or until doubled in bulk.

Bake at 375° for 20 minutes. Combine egg white and 1 tablespoon water; brush mixture on bread, and bake an additional 10 minutes or until loaf sounds hollow when tapped. Remove from pan immediately, and cool on a wire rack. Yield: 1 loaf.

ORANGE BREAKFAST ROLLUPS

- ⅓ cup firmly packed brown sugar
- ¼ cup orange marmalade
- 2 tablespoons butter or margarine, melted
- ¼ cup sliced almonds, toasted
- 1 (3-ounce) package cream cheese, softened
- 1 tablespoon sugar
- 2 tablespoons raisins (optional)
- 1 (10-ounce) can refrigerated flaky biscuits

Combine first 3 ingredients; spoon into a lightly greased 8-inch square pan. Sprinkle with almonds; set aside.

Combine cream cheese and sugar, beating until smooth. Stir in raisins, if desired.

Separate biscuit dough into 10 portions; roll each portion into a 4-inch circle. Spoon 2 teaspoons cream cheese mixture into center, and fold dough over filling, shaping into a log; pinch seam to seal. Place rolls, seam side up, on brown sugar mixture in pan. Bake on lower oven rack at 350° for 25 to 28 minutes. Cool 3 minutes, and turn out onto a serving plate. Yield: 10 rolls.

Above: The perfect way to begin any day is with a slice of this Raspberry-Cream Cheese Coffee Cake.

RASPBERRY-CREAM CHEESE COFFEE CAKE

2¼ cups all-purpose flour
¾ cup sugar
¾ cup butter or margarine
½ teaspoon baking powder
½ teaspoon baking soda
1 teaspoon almond extract
¾ cup sour cream
1 egg
1 (8-ounce) package cream cheese, softened
¼ cup sugar
2 eggs
⅓ cup raspberry preserves
½ cup sliced almonds

Combine flour and ¾ cup sugar; cut in butter with pastry blender until mixture is crumbly. Reserve 1 cup crumb mixture. Add baking powder and next 4 ingredients to remaining crumb mixture, blending well. Spread mixture on bottom and 2 inches up sides of a greased and floured 10-inch springform pan.

Combine cream cheese, ¼ cup sugar, and 2 eggs, mixing well; spoon over crust. Carefully spoon preserves over cheese filling. Combine 1 cup reserved crumb mixture and almonds; sprinkle over preserves. Bake at 350° for 45 to 55 minutes. Cool 15 minutes; remove sides of pan. Let cool completely. Yield: one 10-inch coffee cake.

117

NO-KNEAD KOLACHES

12 pitted prunes*
⅔ cup water
½ cup milk
¼ cup water
3 tablespoons shortening
3 tablespoons sugar
1½ teaspoons salt
1 package dry yeast
¼ cup warm water (105° to 115°)
1 egg
2¾ to 3¼ cups all-purpose flour
3 to 4 tablespoons finely chopped
   pecans
1 cup sifted powdered sugar
1 to 1½ tablespoons milk
½ teaspoon vanilla extract

Combine prunes and ⅔ cup water in a small saucepan; bring to a boil. Reduce heat and simmer 10 minutes. Drain and cool.

Combine ½ cup milk, ¼ cup water, shortening, sugar, and salt in a saucepan; cook over low heat until shortening melts, stirring occasionally. Cool to 110° to 115°.

Dissolve yeast in ¼ cup warm water in a large bowl; let stand 5 minutes. Stir in milk mixture, egg, and enough flour to make a medium-stiff dough.

Turn dough out onto a heavily floured surface; roll to ½-inch thickness. Cut with a 2½-inch round cutter; place on greased baking sheets. Cover and let rise in a warm place (85°), free from drafts, 1 hour or until doubled in bulk.

Make an indentation in center of each circle using the handle of a wooden spoon. Roll each prune in pecans, and press 1 into each indentation. Bake at 350° for 15 to 18 minutes or until lightly browned.

Combine powdered sugar, 1 to 1½ tablespoons milk, and vanilla; drizzle over warm kolaches. Yield: 1 dozen.

*You may substitute dried apricots for prunes, if desired. Combine apricots and ⅓ cup water (instead of ⅔ cup used for prunes) in a small saucepan; bring to a boil, reduce heat, and simmer 20 minutes. Drain and cool.

MIXED FRUIT LOAVES

½ cup chopped dried apricots
½ cup chopped dates
½ cup golden raisins
½ cup rum
2 cups all-purpose flour
1½ teaspoons baking powder
½ teaspoon baking soda
¼ teaspoon salt
1 cup sugar
¼ cup bran cereal
2 eggs, slightly beaten
½ cup butter or margarine, melted
1½ teaspoons buttermilk
1 teaspoon lemon juice
3 medium bananas, mashed
½ cup chopped pecans

Combine first 4 ingredients; cover and let stand 8 hours.

Combine flour and next 5 ingredients; set aside. Combine eggs and next 4 ingredients in a large bowl; add flour mixture, stirring just until dry ingredients are moistened. Fold in pecans and fruit mixture.

Spoon batter into 2 greased and floured 8½- x 4½- x 2½-inch loafpans. Shielding top with aluminum foil if necessary, bake at 350° for 40 to 45 minutes or until a wooden pick inserted in center comes out clean. Cool in pans 10 minutes; remove from pans, and let cool completely on wire racks. Yield: 2 loaves.

Note: Loaves may be frozen up to 2 months.

Tip: Baked yeast bread can be frozen up to 3 months, but raw dough should not be frozen unless specified. Before freezing baked bread, let it cool completely on a wire rack away from drafts, to prevent a soggy bottom and shrinkage. Wrap bread in aluminum foil, and seal tightly in a plastic bag; then label, date, and freeze it. Let foil-wrapped bread thaw at room temperature for 2 to 3 hours, and reheat briefly if desired. Or to reheat frozen bread, bake foil-wrapped bread straight from the freezer at 350° for 20 to 30 minutes.

Confections

DOUBLE-CHOCOLATE CHEESECAKE SQUARES

1¾ cups chocolate wafer crumbs
⅓ cup butter or margarine, melted
   Vegetable cooking spray
4 (6-ounce) white chocolate-flavored
   baking bars, divided*
2 (8-ounce) packages cream cheese,
   softened
½ cup sour cream
4 eggs
2 teaspoons vanilla extract
¼ cup whipping cream
2 tablespoons Frangelica

Combine chocolate wafer crumbs and melted butter; set aside 2 tablespoons mixture. Press remaining crumb mixture onto bottom of a 13- x 9- x 2-inch pan lined with heavy-duty aluminum foil and coated with vegetable cooking spray.

Place 16 ounces white chocolate in top of a double boiler; bring water to a boil. Reduce heat to low; cook until chocolate melts. Let cool slightly.

Combine cream cheese and sour cream in a large mixing bowl; beat at medium speed of an electric mixer until fluffy. Add eggs, one at a time, beating after each addition. Add vanilla and melted chocolate, stirring just until blended.

Pour filling into prepared pan; bake at 300° for 30 minutes; turn oven off, and leave in oven 30 minutes. Cool on wire rack.

Place 8 ounces white chocolate in top of a double boiler; bring water to a boil. Reduce heat to low; cook until chocolate melts. Remove from heat; stir in whipping cream and Frangelica. Pour mixture over cheesecake. Sprinkle with reserved 2 tablespoons crumb mixture. Cover and chill at least 8 hours.

Lift cheesecake from pan, and remove foil. Cut into squares. Yield: 4 dozen.

*You may substitute 24 ounces white chocolate, if desired.

Note: Cheesecake may be frozen up to 1 month in pan. Cover tightly with heavy-duty aluminum foil; freeze. To serve, remove frozen cheesecake from pan; thaw and cut into squares.

Above: Bite-size Double-Chocolate Cheesecake Squares are perfect for parties as well as gift-giving.

OATMEAL-NUT-CHOCOLATE CHIP COOKIES

1½ cups regular oats, uncooked
1 cup butter or margarine, softened
1 cup sugar
1 cup firmly packed brown sugar
2 eggs
1 tablespoon vanilla extract
2 cups all-purpose flour
1 teaspoon baking soda
½ teaspoon baking powder
½ teaspoon salt
1 (12-ounce) package semisweet chocolate morsels
3 (1.5-ounce) bars milk chocolate, grated
1½ cups chopped pecans
12 ounces chocolate-flavored candy coating, melted (optional)

Place oats in container of an electric blender; process until finely ground. Set aside.

Beat butter in a large bowl at medium speed of an electric mixer; gradually add sugars, beating well. Add eggs and vanilla, mixing well.

Combine ground oats, flour, soda, baking powder, and salt; gradually add to creamed mixture, mixing well. Stir in chocolate morsels, grated chocolate, and pecans.

Drop dough by heaping teaspoonfuls onto greased cookie sheets. Bake at 375° for 10 to 12 minutes or until lightly browned. Cool slightly; remove to wire racks to allow to cool completely.

If desired, dip half of each cookie in candy coating; place on wax paper to cool. Yield: about 9 dozen.

RIBBON COOKIES

1 cup butter or margarine, softened
1½ cups sugar
1 egg
1 teaspoon vanilla extract
¼ teaspoon almond extract
2½ cups all-purpose flour
1½ teaspoons baking powder
½ teaspoon salt
½ cup finely chopped candied red cherries, divided
1 (1-ounce) square unsweetened chocolate, melted
¼ cup chopped almonds

Line bottom and sides of a 9- x 5- x 3-inch loafpan with aluminum foil; set loafpan aside.

Beat butter in a large mixing bowl at medium speed of an electric mixer. Gradually add sugar, beating well. Add egg and flavorings; mix well. Combine flour, baking powder, and salt; gradually add to creamed mixture, mixing until blended. (Dough will be stiff.)

Divide dough into thirds. Add half of cherries to one-third of dough; mix well. Press into prepared pan. Knead chocolate and almonds into another third of dough; press over cherry layer. Add remaining cherries to remaining dough; press over chocolate layer. Cover and chill at least 8 hours.

Invert pan, and remove dough. Remove foil. Cut dough lengthwise into thirds. Cut each section of dough crosswise into ¼-inch slices. Place 1 inch apart on ungreased cookie sheets. Bake at 350° for 10 to 12 minutes. Cool on wire racks. Yield: about 7 dozen.

Opposite: The tasty treats shown here are sure to be a hit at any cookie swap. In fact, you may continue to be asked to make them long after the holidays are over. Oatmeal-Nut-Chocolate Chip Cookies are dipped in candy coating. Cherries flavor Christmas Bell Cookies and Ribbon Cookies.

CHRISTMAS BELL COOKIES

- ⅔ cup butter or margarine, softened
- ¾ cup sugar
- 1 egg
- 1 teaspoon grated orange rind
- 1 teaspoon vanilla extract
- 2 cups all-purpose flour
- 1½ teaspoons baking powder
- 30 maraschino cherries, halved

Beat butter at medium speed of an electric mixer; gradually add sugar, beating well. Add egg, orange rind, and vanilla; beat well. Combine flour and baking powder; add to creamed mixture, beating until blended. Cover and chill 30 minutes. Shape dough into two 8-inch rolls. Wrap rolls, and chill at least 8 hours.

Cut rolls into ¼-inch slices; place on ungreased cookie sheets. Place a cherry half on bottom half of each slice; fold in sides, overlapping and slightly covering cherry to resemble a bell. Bake at 350° for 10 to 12 minutes. Cool on wire racks. Yield: 5 dozen.

FROSTED BOURBON BROWNIES

- ½ cup sugar
- ⅓ cup butter or margarine
- 2 tablespoons water
- 1 cup semisweet chocolate morsels
- ¼ cup bourbon
- 1 teaspoon vanilla extract
- 2 eggs
- ¾ cup all-purpose flour
- ¼ teaspoon baking soda
- ¼ teaspoon salt
- 1 cup coarsely chopped walnuts or pecans
- ½ cup butter or margarine, softened
- 2 cups sifted powdered sugar
- 1 teaspoon vanilla extract
- 1 cup semisweet chocolate morsels
- 1 tablespoon butter or margarine

Combine first 3 ingredients in a saucepan; bring to a boil. Remove from heat, and add 1

cup chocolate morsels, bourbon, and 1 teaspoon vanilla, stirring until morsels melt. Add eggs, one at a time, stirring until blended. Combine flour, soda, and salt; add to chocolate mixture, mixing well. Stir in walnuts. Spoon batter into a greased 9-inch square pan. Bake at 325° for 25 to 30 minutes; let brownies cool in pan.

Combine ½ cup butter, powdered sugar, and 1 teaspoon vanilla; beat at medium speed of an electric mixer until smooth. Spread over brownie layer. Cover and chill.

Combine 1 cup chocolate morsels and 1 tablespoon butter in a small heavy saucepan. Cook over low heat until chocolate melts, stirring constantly. Spread over frosting; cover and chill. Cut into squares. Yield: 3 dozen.

BAKLAVA LOGS

- 1 (17¼-ounce) package frozen phyllo pastry, thawed
  About 1¼ cups butter or margarine, melted
- 1 cup ground pecans
- 1 cup ground walnuts
- 1 cup ground almonds
- ¼ cup sugar
- 1 teaspoon ground cinnamon
- 1 teaspoon ground nutmeg
  Honey-Orange Syrup

Cut phyllo in half crosswise to make 14- x 9-inch pieces; cover with a slightly damp towel. Place 1 sheet of phyllo on a damp towel (keep remaining phyllo covered). Lightly brush phyllo with melted butter. Layer 6 sheets of phyllo on first sheet, brushing each with butter.

Combine pecans and next 5 ingredients; sprinkle ½ cup mixture over phyllo stack. Carefully roll phyllo jellyroll fashion, beginning with long side; cut into 1½-inch pieces. Place in a 13- x 9- x 2-inch pan. Repeat procedure 5 times with remaining phyllo sheets and nut mixture.

Bake at 350° for 40 minutes; cool thoroughly. Drizzle warm Honey-Orange Syrup over pastries. Let stand at room temperature 24 hours. Yield: 4½ dozen.

Honey-Orange Syrup:

¾ cup honey
½ cup water
1 tablespoon orange juice concentrate
1 teaspoon grated orange rind

Combine all ingredients in a small saucepan. Bring to a boil; reduce heat, and simmer, uncovered, 5 minutes. Yield: about 1 cup.

PEACH-CREAM CHEESE COOKIES

1 cup butter or margarine, softened
1 (8-ounce) package cream cheese, softened
1½ cups sugar
2 eggs
1½ teaspoons grated lemon rind
2 tablespoons lemon juice
4½ cups all-purpose flour
1½ teaspoons baking powder
¾ cup peach preserves, divided

Cream butter and cream cheese in a large mixing bowl; gradually add sugar, beating at medium speed of an electric mixer. Add eggs, lemon rind, and lemon juice, beating well.

Combine flour and baking powder; add to creamed mixture, and mix well. Chill dough at least 2 hours.

Shape dough into 1-inch balls; place about 2 inches apart on ungreased cookie sheets. Press thumb in center of each cookie leaving an indentation. Fill indentation with about ¼ teaspoon preserves. Bake at 350° for 15 minutes or until lightly browned. Cool on wire racks. Yield: 7 dozen.

EGGNOG CRESCENTS

1 cup butter or margarine, softened
½ cup sifted powdered sugar
2 cups all-purpose flour
1 cup ground almonds
¼ teaspoon salt
¼ to ½ teaspoon rum extract
Rum Glaze
Ground nutmeg

Beat butter in a large mixing bowl at medium speed of an electric mixer; gradually add powdered sugar, beating well.

Combine flour, almonds, and salt; add to creamed mixture, mixing well. Stir in rum extract.

Shape dough into 1-inch balls; shape each ball into a crescent, and place 1 inch apart on ungreased cookie sheets. Bake at 325° for 12 to 15 minutes. Cool on wire racks. Drizzle with Rum Glaze, and sprinkle with nutmeg. Yield: 3½ dozen.

Rum Glaze:

¾ cup sifted powdered sugar
1½ tablespoons milk
⅛ teaspoon rum extract

Combine sifted powdered sugar, milk, and rum extract, stirring until smooth. Yield: about ⅓ cup.

PEPPERMINT CANDY CUPS

12 ounces vanilla-flavored candy coating
¾ cup crushed hard peppermint candy

Place candy coating in a microwave-safe bowl; microwave at MEDIUM (50% power) 4 minutes, stirring after 2 minutes. Stir in candy, and spoon mixture into petit four paper cups. Chill until firm. Store in an airtight container. Yield: 3 dozen.

MARTHA WASHINGTON CANDY

½ cup butter or margarine, softened
⅔ cup sweetened condensed milk
1 (16-ounce) package powdered sugar, sifted
4 cups flaked coconut
2 cups chopped pecans
1 tablespoon lemon juice
1½ teaspoons vanilla extract
1 (24-ounce) package vanilla-flavored candy coating, melted

Beat butter at medium speed of an electric mixer; add condensed milk and next 5 ingredients, beating well. Shape mixture into ¾-inch balls; chill until firm. Dip balls in candy coating, and place on wax paper to cool. Yield: 9 dozen.

COCOA-COFFEE BONBONS

2 cups cream-filled chocolate sandwich cookie crumbs
1 cup chopped pecans
½ cup sifted powdered sugar
2 tablespoons cocoa
2 tablespoons light corn syrup
⅓ cup Kahlúa or other coffee-flavored liqueur
8 ounces chocolate-flavored candy coating, melted

Combine first 5 ingredients; stir in Kahlúa. Cover and chill 1 hour. Shape mixture into 1-inch balls; store in an airtight container 12 hours.
Dip bonbons in candy coating, and place on wax paper to cool. Yield: 3 dozen.

RED CURRANT-FUDGE BALLS

1 (6-ounce) package semisweet chocolate morsels
1 (8-ounce) package cream cheese, softened
¾ cup vanilla wafer crumbs
¼ cup red currant jelly
⅔ cup finely ground almonds, toasted
5 to 6 (2-ounce) squares chocolate-flavored candy coating, melted

Melt chocolate morsels in a heavy saucepan over low heat, stirring constantly; cool slightly.
Combine cream cheese and chocolate; beat at medium speed of an electric mixer until blended. Stir in vanilla wafer crumbs, jelly, and almonds; cover and chill at least 2 hours. Shape mixture into 1-inch balls; cover and chill until firm.
Dip balls in candy coating, and place on wax paper to cool completely. Store in refrigerator. Yield: 3 dozen.

CARAMEL-NUT ROUNDS

½ pound caramels (about 28 pieces)
¼ cup butter or margarine
2 tablespoons milk
1½ cups sifted powdered sugar
1 cup peanuts
2 cups miniature marshmallows
1 (3½-ounce) can flaked coconut

Combine first 3 ingredients in a 2-quart microwave-safe bowl. Microwave at MEDIUM (50% power) 4 to 6 minutes or until melted, stirring after 2 minutes and then at 1-minute intervals. Stir in powdered sugar. Add peanuts and marshmallows, stirring just until blended.
Sprinkle coconut on two 16- x 12-inch sheets of wax paper; spoon half of candy mixture onto each sheet. Shape into two 12-inch logs, coating well with coconut. Wrap and chill several hours. Cut into ½-inch slices. Yield: 4 dozen.

Festive Desserts

APPLE SYLLABUB DESSERT

½ cup superfine sugar
¼ cup apple butter
2 tablespoons apple brandy
2¾ teaspoons lemon juice
¼ teaspoon ground cinnamon
⅛ teaspoon ground nutmeg
2 cups whipping cream
1 (3-ounce) package ladyfingers, split
   Ground nutmeg

Combine first 6 ingredients; set aside. Beat whipping cream at high speed of an electric mixer until soft peaks form. Set aside ½ cup whipped cream. Fold remaining whipped cream into apple mixture. Line a 1½-quart bowl with ladyfingers. Spoon in apple mixture. Garnish with reserved whipped cream; sprinkle with nutmeg. Yield: 6 to 8 servings.

CHOCOLATE MOUSSE TARTS

24 vanilla wafers
1 (8-ounce) package cream cheese, softened
1 (3-ounce) package cream cheese, softened
⅔ cup sugar
6 eggs
⅓ cup whipping cream
1 tablespoon vanilla extract
8 (1-ounce) squares semisweet chocolate, melted
   Sweetened whipped cream
   Chocolate syrup
   Garnish: maraschino cherries with stems (optional)

Line muffin pans with paper liners. Place a vanilla wafer in each liner; set aside.

Beat cream cheese and sugar in a large mixing bowl at medium speed of an electric mixer

Above: Garnished with whipped cream and cherries, Chocolate Mousse Tarts are a festive variation on the ever-popular chocolate cheesecake.

until light and fluffy. Add eggs, one at a time, beating after each addition. Add whipping cream, vanilla, and melted chocolate; beat at low speed just until blended. Spoon mixture into liners. Bake at 325° for 14 to 16 minutes. Remove from oven, and cool in pans on a wire rack. Cover and chill.

Before serving, pipe or dollop sweetened whipped cream in centers of tarts; drizzle with chocolate syrup. Garnish, if desired. Yield: 2 dozen.

CRANBERRY-APPLE TARTS

     Pastry for double-crust 9-inch pie
4 cups fresh cranberries
1¾ cups peeled, chopped cooking apples
2½ cups sugar
½ cup water
2 tablespoons cornstarch
2 tablespoons water
½ cup chopped pecans
1 tablespoon grated orange rind
1 tablespoon butter or margarine,
    melted
    Sweetened whipped cream

Fit pastry into eight 4-inch tart pans. Reserve remaining pastry for garnish.

Combine cranberries, apples, sugar, and ½ cup water in a saucepan. Bring to a boil; reduce heat, and simmer 10 minutes. Combine cornstarch and 2 tablespoons water; stir into cranberry mixture, and cook over low heat 2 minutes. Let cool. Stir in pecans and orange rind. Spoon filling into prepared pastry shells. Bake at 425° for 15 to 20 minutes. Let cool completely.

Using a fluted pastry wheel, cut thirty-two 3- x ½-inch strips from remaining pastry; pinch ends of 16 strips together to look like loops of a bow. Place loops and remaining strips on ungreased baking sheet, and bake at 425° for 10 minutes or until lightly browned. Brush with melted butter, and allow to cool completely.

Place 2 loops and 2 strips on each tart to form bow; pipe whipped cream on bow. Yield: 8 servings.

Note: Tarts can be frozen after assembly; thaw and serve.

PUMPKIN ICE-CREAM PIE

  1 cup cooked, mashed pumpkin
½ cup firmly packed brown sugar
½ teaspoon ground ginger
½ teaspoon ground cinnamon
¼ teaspoon ground nutmeg
1½ quarts vanilla ice cream, softened and
    divided
  1 (9-inch) Gingersnap Crumb Crust
    Butterscotch Sauce

Combine first 5 ingredients, stirring until sugar dissolves. Stir in 1 quart ice cream. Spoon mixture into prepared crust; freeze 2 hours. Spread remaining ½ quart ice cream over pie; freeze. Serve with Butterscotch Sauce. Yield: one 9-inch pie.

Gingersnap Crumb Crust:

1½ cups gingersnap crumbs
½ cup sifted powdered sugar
⅓ cup butter or margarine, melted

Combine all ingredients; firmly press mixture evenly over bottom and sides of a 9-inch pie-plate. Bake at 375° for 4 to 5 minutes; cool. Yield: one 9-inch crust.

Butterscotch Sauce:

1 cup firmly packed brown sugar
⅓ cup light corn syrup
2 tablespoons butter or margarine
¼ cup half-and-half

Combine first 3 ingredients in a 1-quart glass measure; microwave at HIGH 2 to 3 minutes, stirring twice. Stir in half-and-half. Serve warm. Yield: 1½ cups.

Opposite: A tasty blend of tangy cranberries and mellow apples goes into these Cranberry-Apple Tarts. The rich red filling, accented with a pastry bow, makes them almost too pretty to eat. For easy party planning, they can be made ahead and frozen.

ALABAMA CHOCOLATE-PECAN JUMBO CHRISTMAS FUDGE PIE

1¼ cups chocolate wafer crumbs
⅓ cup butter or margarine, melted
½ cup butter or margarine, softened
¾ cup firmly packed brown sugar
3 eggs
1 (12-ounce) package semisweet chocolate morsels, melted
2 teaspoons instant coffee granules
1 teaspoon vanilla extract
½ cup all-purpose flour
1 cup coarsely chopped pecans
Sweetened whipped cream
Chocolate syrup
Garnishes: maraschino cherries with stems, mint sprigs (optional)

Combine wafer crumbs and ⅓ cup melted butter; firmly press mixture on bottom and sides of a 9-inch tart pan or pieplate. Bake at 350° for 6 to 8 minutes.

Beat ½ cup butter in a large mixing bowl at medium speed of an electric mixer; gradually add brown sugar, beating until blended. Add eggs, one at a time, beating after each addition. Stir in melted chocolate and next 4 ingredients. Pour mixture into prepared crust. Bake at 375° for 25 minutes; cool completely on a wire rack.

Before serving, pipe sweetened whipped cream on top of each serving, and drizzle with chocolate syrup. Garnish, if desired. Yield: one 9-inch pie.

WHITE CHOCOLATE TERRINE WITH CRANBERRY SAUCE

3 cups whipping cream
¼ cup butter
4 egg yolks, beaten
12 ounces white chocolate, melted*
Cranberry Sauce

Combine whipping cream and butter in a large saucepan; cook over low heat until butter melts. Gradually stir about one-fourth of hot mixture into yolks; add to remaining hot mixture, stirring constantly. Stir in melted chocolate. Pour mixture into a lightly greased 8½- x 4½- x 3-inch loafpan. Place loafpan in a large shallow pan. Pour hot water to a depth of 1 inch in pan. Bake, covered, at 350° for 1½ hours (center will not be firm). Remove from hot water, and cool. Cover and chill at least 8 hours.

Before serving, spoon 2 tablespoons Cranberry Sauce onto individual plates; top with a slice of chocolate terrine. Yield: 14 servings.

*Vanilla-flavored candy coating should not be substituted in this recipe.

Cranberry Sauce:

¼ cup sugar
2 tablespoons cornstarch
1 (12-ounce) can frozen cranberry juice cocktail, thawed
½ cup water

Combine sugar and cornstarch in a heavy saucepan. Stir in thawed cranberry juice and water. Cook over medium heat until mixture comes to a boil. Boil 1 minute; remove from heat. Cover and chill thoroughly. Yield: about 2 cups.

CINNAMON TORTILLAS WITH ICE CREAM

⅓ cup sugar
2 teaspoons ground cinnamon
Vegetable oil
6 (6-inch) flour tortillas
1 quart vanilla ice cream
Cinnamon Sauce

Combine sugar and cinnamon; set aside. Pour oil to a depth of 3 inches into a medium

128

saucepan, 1 to 1½ inches smaller than the diameter of the tortilla; heat to 375°. Push tortilla into oil using a metal ladle, pressing down in center. Cook 45 to 60 seconds or until golden brown. Drain. Sprinkle sugar mixture over warm tortillas.

To serve, place each tortilla cup on serving plate; top with a scoop of ice cream. Drizzle with Cinnamon Sauce. Yield: 6 servings.

Cinnamon Sauce:

¼ cup sugar
1 tablespoon cornstarch
1 cup water
3 tablespoons lemon juice
1 tablespoon butter or margarine
1 teaspoon ground cinnamon
½ teaspoon ground nutmeg

Combine sugar and cornstarch in a small saucepan; add water and lemon juice, stirring well. Cook over medium heat, stirring constantly, until mixture thickens. Add butter, cinnamon, and nutmeg. Serve warm over ice cream. Yield: 1 cup.

KAHLÚA SOUFFLÉS

Butter or margarine
1 tablespoon sugar
Kahlúa Sauce
¼ cup butter or margarine
¼ cup all-purpose flour
1 cup milk
4 eggs, separated
2 tablespoons Kahlúa
¾ cup sugar
2 tablespoons cornstarch
Powdered sugar

Lightly butter ten 6-ounce custard cups, and sprinkle bottom and sides of cups evenly with 1 tablespoon sugar. Spoon Kahlúa Sauce evenly into each cup.

Melt ¼ cup butter in a large saucepan over low heat; add flour, stirring until mixture is smooth. Cook, stirring constantly, 1 minute. Gradually stir in milk and cook, stirring constantly, until mixture thickens and begins to leave sides of pan.

Remove from heat, and let cool about 15 minutes. Add egg yolks to mixture, one at a time, beating after each addition. Stir Kahlúa into sauce mixture; set aside.

Combine ¾ cup sugar and cornstarch; set aside. Beat egg whites in a large mixing bowl at medium speed of an electric mixer until foamy. Slowly add sugar mixture; beat until stiff but not dry. Gradually stir about one-fourth of sauce mixture into egg whites; gently fold into remaining sauce mixture.

Spoon mixture over Kahlúa Sauce in custard cups; place cups in a large shallow pan. Pour hot water to a depth of 1 inch in pan. Bake at 400° for 10 minutes. Reduce oven temperature to 350°, and bake an additional 20 to 25 minutes or until tops are golden brown.

Remove custard cups from water; sprinkle with powdered sugar, and serve immediately. Yield: 10 servings.

Note: To make ahead, use only freezer-to-oven dishes. Wrap individual dishes in heavy-duty foil; freeze up to 2 weeks. When ready to serve, remove soufflés from freezer; place in shallow pan. Pour hot water to a depth of 1 inch in pan. Bake at 400° for 10 minutes; reduce temperature to 350°, and bake an additional 40 minutes or until golden brown. Sprinkle soufflés with powdered sugar, and serve immediately.

Kahlúa Sauce:

⅓ cup water
⅓ cup sugar
3 tablespoons light corn syrup
¼ cup cocoa
2 tablespoons Kahlúa

Combine first 3 ingredients in a small saucepan; bring to a boil. Boil 1 minute, stirring constantly. Remove from heat, and stir in cocoa and Kahlúa. Yield: ¾ cup.

WINTER FRUIT CRISP

3 cooking apples, unpeeled and sliced
   (about 1½ pounds)
2 cups fresh cranberries
1 (8-ounce) can unsweetened crushed
   pineapple, undrained
½ cup sugar
1 cup firmly packed brown sugar
¼ cup all-purpose flour
½ cup butter or margarine, softened
1 cup regular oats, uncooked
1 cup chopped pecans
   Sweetened whipped cream

Layer apples, cranberries, and pineapple in a lightly greased 13- x 9- x 2-inch baking dish; sprinkle with ½ cup sugar, and set aside.

Combine brown sugar and flour; cut in butter with a pastry blender. Stir in oats and pecans. Sprinkle mixture over fruit. Cover and refrigerate 8 hours. Remove from refrigerator; let stand 30 minutes. Uncover and bake at 375° for 30 minutes. Serve with whipped cream. Yield: 8 to 10 servings.

APPLE CAKE
WITH CARAMEL SAUCE

3 cooking apples, peeled, cored, and
   quartered
½ cup butter or margarine, softened
1 cup sugar
1 egg
1 cup all-purpose flour
1 teaspoon baking soda
¼ teaspoon salt
1 teaspoon ground cinnamon
¾ teaspoon ground nutmeg
½ cup chopped pecans
   Caramel Sauce
   Garnishes: sweetened whipped
     cream, apple slices (optional)

Position knife blade in food processor bowl; add 4 apple quarters. Cover with top; process 20 seconds or until apple is finely chopped. Repeat procedure twice, using enough remaining apple quarters to make 2½ cups chopped apple. Set aside.

Beat butter in a large bowl at medium speed of an electric mixer. Gradually add sugar, beating well. Add egg; mix well. Combine flour and next 4 ingredients; add to creamed mixture, stirring until blended. Stir in chopped apple and pecans.

Spoon batter into a greased and floured paper-lined 9- x 5- x 3-inch loafpan. Bake at 350° for 40 to 45 minutes or until a wooden pick inserted in center comes out clean. Cool in pan 10 minutes; remove from pan, and let cool completely on a wire rack. Serve with Caramel Sauce. Garnish, if desired. Yield: one 9-inch loaf.

Caramel Sauce:

½ cup butter or margarine, melted
1 cup firmly packed brown sugar
1 teaspoon vanilla extract
1 (5-ounce) can evaporated milk

Combine butter and brown sugar in a saucepan; bring to a boil over medium-low heat, stirring constantly. Remove from heat. Stir in vanilla and evaporated milk. Yield: 1 cup.

LEMON CHEESECAKES

   Butter or margarine
4 teaspoons graham cracker crumbs
1 (8-ounce) package cream cheese
½ cup sour cream
¼ cup sugar
1 egg
1½ teaspoons all-purpose flour
½ teaspoon grated lemon rind
1 teaspoon lemon juice
½ teaspoon vanilla extract
   Lemon Sauce
   Garnish: strawberries (optional)

Lightly butter four 6-ounce custard cups; coat bottom and sides of cups with graham cracker crumbs. Set aside.

Place cream cheese in a 3-quart microwave-safe mixing bowl; microwave, uncovered, at MEDIUM (50% power) 1 to 1½ minutes or until cream cheese is softened. Add sour cream and next 6 ingredients; beat at medium speed of an electric mixer until blended. Spoon mixture into prepared custard cups.

Arrange custard cups in a ring in a 9-inch pieplate. Microwave, uncovered, at MEDIUM 4 minutes, giving plate a half-turn after 2 minutes to rotate custard cups. Microwave, uncovered, at HIGH 1 to 2 minutes or until centers are set, checking for doneness every 30 seconds after 1 minute.

Cool 30 minutes on a wire rack. Loosen edges of cheesecakes, and remove from custard cups. Cover and chill. To serve, spoon Lemon Sauce over each cheesecake and garnish, if desired. Yield: 4 servings.

Lemon Sauce:

¼ cup sugar
2¼ teaspoons cornstarch
½ cup water
¾ teaspoon grated lemon rind
2½ tablespoons lemon juice
1½ teaspoons butter or margarine

Combine sugar and cornstarch in a 2-cup glass measure; add water, stirring until sugar dissolves. Microwave at HIGH 2 to 3 minutes, stirring at 1-minute intervals until mixture is thickened and bubbly. Stir in next three ingredients. Cover and chill. Yield: ¾ cup.

Tip: Most baked cake layers can be frozen up to two months before frosting and serving. Let layers cool completely on a wire rack; seal them in an airtight freezer bag; label, date, and freeze. Thaw wrapped frozen layers at room temperature about four hours. Frost cake while layers are still cold, if possible.

ITALIAN CREAM CAKE

(pictured on page 99)

½ cup butter or margarine, softened
½ cup shortening
2 cups sugar
5 eggs
2 cups all-purpose flour
1 teaspoon baking soda
1 cup buttermilk
1 teaspoon vanilla extract
1 (3½-ounce) can flaked coconut
1 cup chopped pecans
Cream Cheese Frosting

Beat butter and shortening in a large mixing bowl at medium speed of an electric mixer; gradually add sugar, beating well. Add eggs, one at a time, beating after each addition.

Combine flour and soda; add to creamed mixture alternately with buttermilk, beginning and ending with flour mixture. Mix after each addition. Stir in vanilla, coconut, and pecans.

Pour batter into 3 greased and floured 9-inch round cakepans. Bake at 350° for 20 to 25 minutes or until a wooden pick inserted in center comes out clean. Cool in pans 10 minutes; remove from pans, and let cool completely on wire racks.

Spread Cream Cheese Frosting between layers and on top and sides of cake. Yield: one 3-layer cake.

Cream Cheese Frosting:

⅓ cup butter or margarine, softened
1 (8-ounce) package cream cheese, softened
1 (3-ounce) package cream cheese, softened
6½ cups sifted powdered sugar
1½ teaspoons vanilla extract

Cream butter and cream cheese; gradually add powdered sugar, beating until smooth and creamy. Add vanilla, and beat until blended. Yield: enough for one 3-layer cake.

Party Fare

PEPPERED SESAME-CHEESE TWISTS

1 (17¼-ounce) package frozen puff
  pastry, thawed
½ cup grated Parmesan cheese
¼ cup sesame seeds, toasted
  Red pepper

On a lightly floured surface, roll 1 sheet of puff pastry into an 18- x 14-inch rectangle. Sprinkle with 2 tablespoons Parmesan cheese and 1 tablespoon sesame seeds, and gently press toppings into dough with a rolling pin. Fold dough in half crosswise, making a 14- x 9-inch rectangle. Roll dough into an 18- x 14-inch rectangle again. Sprinkle with 2 tablespoons cheese, 1 tablespoon sesame seeds, and a small amount of red pepper; gently press toppings into dough with rolling pin. Repeat process with remaining pastry and toppings.

Cut dough crosswise into ⅔-inch strips. Wind each strip into a corkscrew around the handle of a wooden spoon; gently pull out spoon and place twist on ungreased baking sheet. Bake at 350° for 15 to 20 minutes or until golden brown and crisp. Cool on wire racks, and store in an airtight container. Yield: 4½ dozen appetizers.

Note: For Cinnamon Twists, substitute ⅔ cup sugar and 2 teaspoons ground cinnamon for cheese, sesame seeds, and red pepper.

CHUTNEY-CASHEW SPREAD

1 (8-ounce) package cream cheese,
  softened
1 cup chutney, chopped
1 cup coarsely chopped cashews
⅔ cup sour cream
1 tablespoon curry powder
  Assorted condiments
  Melba toast or endive

Combine first 5 ingredients, and spoon into serving bowl. Arrange several of the following condiments on top: crumbled cooked bacon, flaked coconut, currants, and chopped green onions. Serve with melba toast or endive. Yield: 3 cups.

ROASTED PEPPER STRIPS AND ENDIVE

1 large sweet red pepper
¼ cup olive oil
1½ tablespoons balsamic vinegar
1½ tablespoons minced fresh parsley
¼ teaspoon salt
1 clove garlic, minced
  Pinch of white pepper
6 heads Belgian endive
  Garnish: fresh parsley sprigs
  (optional)

Place pepper on a baking sheet. Bake at 500° for 20 minutes or until skin is blackened and charred. Transfer pepper immediately to a paper bag, and seal top. Refrigerate 10 minutes or until pepper cools. Peel pepper, discarding seeds and charred skin. Cut pepper into 2- x ¼-inch strips. Set aside.

Combine olive oil and next 5 ingredients; add pepper strips. Cover and chill 8 hours. Slice stem end from endive, and separate leaves. Place a pepper strip on each endive leaf. Cover with a damp towel, and refrigerate until ready to serve. Garnish, if desired. Yield: about 30 appetizers.

Opposite: These flavorful party dishes will enhance your holiday menu with unexpected Christmas spices—red pepper and curry. Clockwise from front: Roasted Pepper Strips and Endive, Peppered Sesame-Cheese Twists, and Chutney-Cashew Spread.

BRANDIED PÂTÉ

    8 slices bacon
    1 pound chicken livers
    ½ cup brandy
    ¾ cup whipping cream
    ½ cup chopped onion
    ¼ cup mayonnaise or salad dressing
    1 teaspoon dried whole thyme
      Pinch of ground nutmeg
    ¼ teaspoon salt
    ¼ teaspoon freshly ground pepper
    ½ cup coarsely chopped walnuts
    3 tablespoons chopped fresh parsley
      Garnishes: chopped fresh parsley,
        chopped walnuts (optional)

Cook bacon until crisp in a large skillet; drain and crumble bacon, reserving 2 tablespoons drippings. Set bacon aside.

Sauté livers in reserved drippings until lightly browned. Drain livers, and set aside, reserving drippings in skillet. Remove skillet from heat. Pour brandy into skillet, stirring to loosen particles in pan. Stir in whipping cream; return to heat, and bring to a boil. Reduce heat, and cook over medium heat, stirring constantly, until mixture is reduced to about 1 cup.

Position knife blade in food processor bowl; add cream mixture, livers, and onion. Process 1 minute or until smooth. Add mayonnaise, thyme, nutmeg, salt, and pepper; process until blended. Add reserved bacon, walnuts, and parsley; process 10 seconds.

Pour into a lightly greased 3-cup mold; cover and chill 8 hours. Remove from mold, and garnish, if desired. Serve with assorted crackers. Yield: 3 cups.

SEAFOOD PÂTÉ

    2 envelopes unflavored gelatin
    3 tablespoons cold water
    1 (10¾-ounce) can cream of shrimp
      soup, undiluted
    1 (10½-ounce) can she-crab soup,
      undiluted
    1 (8-ounce) package cream cheese,
      softened
    1 cup diced celery
    ¾ cup mayonnaise or salad dressing
    ⅓ cup dry sherry
    2 tablespoons grated onion
    ¼ teaspoon lemon-pepper seasoning
    1 (6-ounce) can crabmeat, drained
    1 (4-ounce) can medium shrimp,
      drained

Sprinkle gelatin over cold water; set aside. Combine shrimp soup and next 2 ingredients in a large saucepan; cook over low heat until cheese melts, stirring often. Add gelatin mixture, stirring well. Stir in celery and next 4 ingredients. Fold in crabmeat and shrimp.

Spoon into a lightly greased 5-cup mold. Cover and chill 8 hours or until firm. Unmold onto serving plate; serve with crackers. Yield: 5 cups.

TACO CHICKEN DRUMMETTES

    3½ pounds chicken wings
    1 (8-ounce) jar hot taco sauce
    1 cup dry breadcrumbs
    3 tablespoons taco seasoning mix

Cut chicken wings in half at joint; set drummettes aside, and reserve remaining parts for other uses. Combine drummettes and taco sauce in a shallow container; cover and refrigerate 2 hours.

Combine breadcrumbs and seasoning mix. Dredge drummettes in mixture, and place on a lightly greased baking sheet. Bake at 375° for 35 to 40 minutes. Yield: 16 drummettes.

PARTY VEGETABLE SANDWICHES

    1 envelope unflavored gelatin
    ½ cup cold water
    1½ cups mayonnaise or salad dressing
    1 tablespoon lemon juice
    1¾ cups shredded carrot
    1 cup finely chopped celery
    1 large cucumber, diced
    1 small onion, diced
    24 slices very thin white sandwich bread
    12 slices very thin whole wheat
        sandwich bread

Sprinkle gelatin over cold water in a large saucepan; let stand 1 minute. Cook over low heat, stirring until gelatin dissolves. Stir in mayonnaise and lemon juice. Add carrot, celery, cucumber, and onion, stirring until blended. Cover and chill at least 8 hours. Remove mixture from refrigerator; stir well.

Spread 3 tablespoons vegetable mixture on 1 slice white bread. Top with 1 slice whole wheat bread; spread 3 tablespoons vegetable mixture on wheat bread, and top with 1 slice white bread. Repeat procedure with remaining ingredients. Press stacks together firmly, and trim the crusts. Cut each sandwich into 4 triangles. Yield: 4 dozen.

MINI CHEDDAR-WALNUT BALLS

    2 cups (8 ounces) shredded Cheddar
        cheese
    ¼ cup butter or margarine, softened
    1 small clove garlic, crushed
    2 teaspoons Worcestershire sauce
    1¼ cups finely chopped walnuts, divided
        Pretzel sticks (optional)
        Strawberry preserves (optional)

Combine first 4 ingredients and ½ cup walnuts, mixing well. Shape into 1-inch balls, and roll in remaining chopped walnuts. Chill 1 hour. If desired, insert a pretzel or decorative wooden pick into each ball, and serve with strawberry preserves. Yield: 2½ dozen.

CRÈME DE MENTHE SQUARES

    1¼ cups butter or margarine, melted and
        divided
    ½ cup cocoa
    3½ cups sifted powdered sugar, divided
    1 egg, slightly beaten
    1 teaspoon vanilla extract
    2 cups graham cracker crumbs
    ¼ to ⅓ cup green crème de menthe
    1½ cups semisweet chocolate morsels

Combine ½ cup melted butter, cocoa, ½ cup powdered sugar, egg, vanilla, and graham cracker crumbs, stirring until blended. Press mixture onto bottom of an ungreased 13- x 9- x 2-inch pan.

Combine ½ cup melted butter and crème de menthe in a mixing bowl. Gradually add remaining 3 cups powdered sugar, beating at low speed of an electric mixer until smooth. Spread mixture over crumb layer. Chill 1 hour.

Combine remaining ¼ cup melted butter and chocolate morsels in a saucepan; cook over low heat until chocolate melts, stirring constantly. Spread over mint layer. Chill 2 hours. Cut into small squares; store in refrigerator. Yield: 8 dozen.

SPINACH DIP

    1 (10-ounce) package frozen chopped
        spinach, thawed and well drained
    ½ cup sour cream
    ½ cup mayonnaise or salad dressing
    ¼ cup chopped green onions
    1½ teaspoons lemon juice
    ½ teaspoon dried whole dillweed

Combine all ingredients; cover and chill at least 2 hours. Serve with an assortment of fresh vegetables. Yield: 2 cups.

Above: Gifts from the kitchen are always appreciated during the holiday season. Clockwise from left: Cherry Treats, Honeyed Peach Glaze, Herb-and-Pepper Cheese Spread.

Gift Ideas

CHERRY TREATS

½ cup butter or margarine, softened
¾ cup firmly packed dark brown sugar
¾ cup sugar
2 eggs
2 cups all-purpose flour
1 teaspoon baking powder
½ cup maraschino cherry juice
½ cup chopped maraschino cherries
¼ cup chopped pecans
Sifted powdered sugar

Beat butter at medium speed of an electric mixer; gradually add sugars, beating well. Add eggs, beating until blended.

Combine flour and baking powder; add to creamed mixture alternately with cherry juice. Stir in cherries. Spoon into paper-lined miniature (1¾-inch) muffin pans, filling three-fourths full. Sprinkle with pecans. Bake at 400° for 10 to 12 minutes or until lightly browned. Remove from pans, and place on wire racks to cool. Sprinkle with powdered sugar. Yield: 4 dozen.

HONEYED PEACH GLAZE

1 (12-ounce) jar peach preserves
⅓ cup honey
2 teaspoons prepared horseradish
½ teaspoon curry powder
½ teaspoon ground ginger

Combine all ingredients, stirring well; spoon mixture into an airtight container. Store in refrigerator up to 3 months. Yield: 1 cup.

Directions for gift card: Store Honeyed Peach Glaze in refrigerator up to 3 months. Brush glaze over ham, pork, chicken, or Cornish hens during baking, or serve glaze as an appetizer with cream cheese and crackers.

HERB-AND-PEPPER CHEESE SPREAD

2 (8-ounce) packages cream cheese, softened
½ cup butter or margarine, softened
2 teaspoons chopped fresh chives
1 teaspoon dried whole basil
1 teaspoon caraway seeds
1 teaspoon dillseeds
⅓ cup finely chopped sweet red, green, or yellow pepper

Combine first 6 ingredients; beat at medium speed of an electric mixer until smooth. Stir in sweet pepper. Spoon into crocks or airtight containers; refrigerate for up to 1 week. Yield: 2¾ cups.

Directions for gift card: Store Herb-and-Pepper Cheese Spread in refrigerator up to 1 week. Serve with bagel chips or crackers.

BARBECUE SAUCE

1 (32-ounce) bottle catsup
1 (12-ounce) bottle chili sauce
1 (12-ounce) can beer
1¾ cups firmly packed brown sugar
1½ cups white vinegar
1 cup lemon juice
½ cup steak sauce
⅓ cup prepared mustard
¼ cup Worcestershire sauce
2 tablespoons pepper
1 tablespoon dry mustard
2 tablespoons vegetable oil
1 tablespoon soy sauce

Combine all ingredients in a Dutch oven; cook over medium heat 8 minutes, stirring occasionally. Pour mixture into bottles; refrigerate up to 3 months. Yield: 2½ quarts.

Directions for gift card: Store Barbecue Sauce in refrigerator up to 3 months. Use to baste pork or chicken during cooking.

MELON SALSA

½ cup white vinegar
½ cup sugar
1 cup raisins
⅓ cup sliced green onions
1 clove garlic, pressed
½ teaspoon dried whole cilantro
⅛ teaspoon dried red pepper flakes
3 cups finely chopped cantaloupe
1 small jalapeño pepper, seeded and
   finely diced
¼ cup fresh lime juice

Combine vinegar and sugar in a small sauce-pan; bring to a boil, stirring until sugar dissolves. Stir in raisins and next 4 ingredients; cook 3 minutes. Stir in cantaloupe and remaining ingredients. Bring mixture to a boil; remove from heat, and let cool. Spoon into three 1-cup gift containers, and refrigerate up to 2 weeks. Yield: 3 cups.

Directions for gift card: Store Melon Salsa in refrigerator up to 2 weeks. Serve with pork and seafood.

SPICE-GLAZED NUTS

1½ cups pecan halves
1 (8-ounce) package blanched whole
   almonds
⅓ cup sugar
1 teaspoon ground cinnamon
½ teaspoon ground nutmeg
3 tablespoons vegetable oil

Spread pecans and almonds in a 15- x 10- x 1-inch jellyroll pan. Bake at 350° for 8 minutes, stirring once.

Combine sugar, cinnamon, and nutmeg in a large, heavy skillet; add vegetable oil and nuts, stirring to coat. Cook over medium heat 3 to 4 minutes, stirring constantly. Spread nuts in a thin layer on jellyroll pan; cool. Yield: 3 cups.

MICROWAVE MOCHA FUDGE MIX

1 (16-ounce) package powdered sugar,
   sifted
½ cup cocoa
¼ teaspoon salt
1½ teaspoons instant coffee granules
⅛ to ¼ teaspoon ground cinnamon

Combine all ingredients; store in an airtight container. Yield: one 4½-cup gift package.

Directions for gift recipe card: Place Microwave Mocha Fudge Mix in a 2-quart glass bowl; add ½ cup butter or margarine. Microwave at HIGH, uncovered, 2 to 3 minutes; stir until smooth. Stir in ¼ cup milk, 1 teaspoon vanilla extract, and 1 cup chopped pecans. Pour mixture into an 8-inch square baking dish. Refrigerate until firm; cut into squares. Store in refrigerator. Yield: 1½ pounds.

ORANGE-GRAPEFRUIT JELLY

6½ cups sugar
2 cups water
¼ cup plus 2 tablespoons lemon juice
1 (6-ounce) can frozen orange juice
   concentrate, thawed and undiluted
1 (6-ounce) can frozen grapefruit juice
   concentrate, thawed and undiluted
1 (6-ounce) package liquid pectin

Combine sugar and water in a large Dutch oven; bring to a full rolling boil. Add lemon juice, and boil 1 minute. Stir in remaining ingredients; boil 1 minute, stirring constantly. Remove from heat, and skim off foam with a metal spoon.

Quickly pour mixture into hot sterilized jars, leaving ¼-inch of headspace; wipe jar rims. Cover at once with metal lids, and screw on bands. Process in boiling-water bath 5 minutes. Yield: 9 half pints.

Directions for gift card: After opening, keep Orange-Grapefruit Jelly refrigerated.

MINTED COFFEE MIX

¼ cup instant coffee granules
¼ cup powdered non-dairy coffee
   creamer
⅓ cup sugar
2 tablespoons cocoa
1½ tablespoons crushed hard peppermint
   candy (about 2 sticks)

Combine all ingredients in container of an electric blender; process until blended. Store in an airtight container. Yield: 1 cup mix.

Directions for gift recipe card: Combine 2 tablespoons Minted Coffee Mix with 6 ounces boiling water. Yield: 8 servings.

HERB VINAIGRETTE WITH HERB-CHEESE CROUTONS

½ cup olive oil
½ cup vegetable oil
⅓ to ½ cup white wine vinegar
3 tablespoons grated Parmesan cheese
1½ tablespoons Dijon mustard
1 teaspoon dried Italian seasoning
½ teaspoon freshly ground pepper
½ teaspoon dried parsley flakes
1 clove garlic, crushed

Combine all ingredients in container of an electric blender; process until smooth. Store in refrigerator up to 3 months. Yield: 1½ cups.

Herb-Cheese Croutons:

1 (13-ounce) package small soft
   breadsticks
¼ cup olive oil
¼ cup butter or margarine, melted
2 cloves garlic, minced
¼ cup grated Parmesan cheese
2 teaspoons dried Italian seasoning
¼ teaspoon red pepper

Slice bread with a serrated knife into ⅜-inch-thick rounds. Combine olive oil, butter, and

Above: For a zesty gift, fill decorative bottles with Herb Vinaigrette. Include a box of homemade Herb-Cheese Croutons to complete the package.

garlic; drizzle over bread slices, tossing to coat. Combine Parmesan cheese, Italian seasoning, and red pepper; sprinkle over bread slices, tossing to coat.

Place on baking sheet; bake at 400° for 5 minutes. Turn slices over, and bake an additional 2 to 5 minutes or until crisp and golden brown. Cool and store in an airtight container for up to 3 weeks. Yield: 10 cups.

Directions for gift card: Store Herb Vinaigrette in refrigerator up to 3 months; shake before serving. Store Herb-Cheese Croutons in an airtight container up to 3 weeks. Toss vinaigrette with salad greens just before serving, and top with croutons.

Patterns

Perforated Paper Snowflakes

Instructions are on page 84.
Cross-Stitch Charts

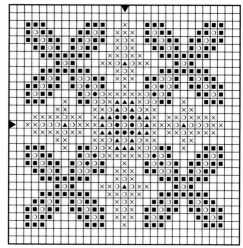

White Paper Square

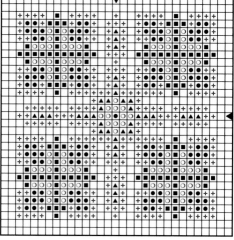

Red Paper Square

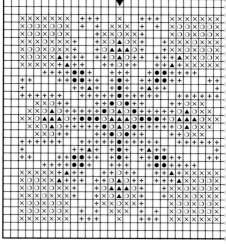

Green Paper Square

GOLD SNOWFLAKE

Cut 1 from each gold perforated paper square.

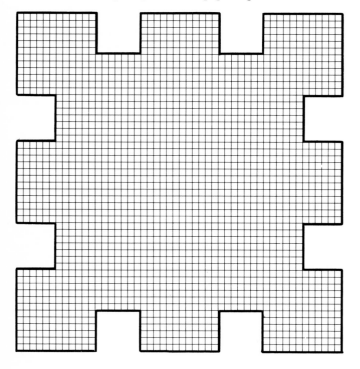

COLOR KEY

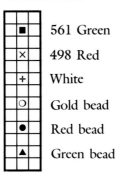

■	561 Green
×	498 Red
+	White
○	Gold bead
●	Red bead
▲	Green bead

(*Note:* Numbers are for DMC floss.)

Use 3 strands of floss and 1 strand of blending filament for all cross-stitching. Use quilting thread to attach beads.

Etched Snowflakes Are Easy And Elegant

Instructions are on page 74.

Cut out white areas of stencil.

Cutting line

Oodles of Noodles

MACARONI LAMB
Instructions are on page 95.
Patterns are full-size.

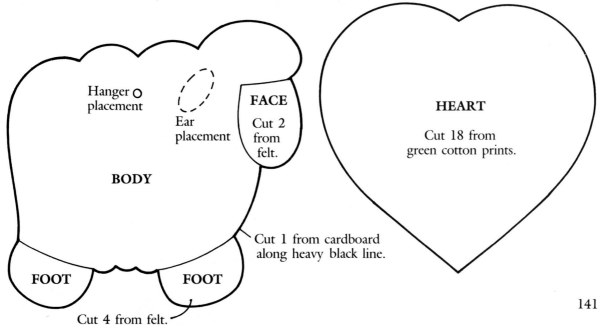

Hanger placement

Ear placement

FACE
Cut 2 from felt.

BODY

Cut 1 from cardboard along heavy black line.

FOOT   **FOOT**

Cut 4 from felt.

Quilt a Tree of Hearts

Instructions are on page 87.
Pattern is full-size and includes ¼″ seam allowance.

HEART

Cut 18 from green cotton prints.

141

A Nativity in the Round

Instructions are on page 75.

Patterns are
full-size.

Cut patterns from pine shelving along heavy
black lines.

Transfer details of each figure onto both sides of
wood and trace with brown permanent marker.

Cutting line

Cutting line

Cutting line

Cutting line

Cutting line

Cutting line

Cutting line

Cutting line

Cutting line

Cutting line

143

Package Toppers

Instructions are on page 90.
Patterns are full-size.

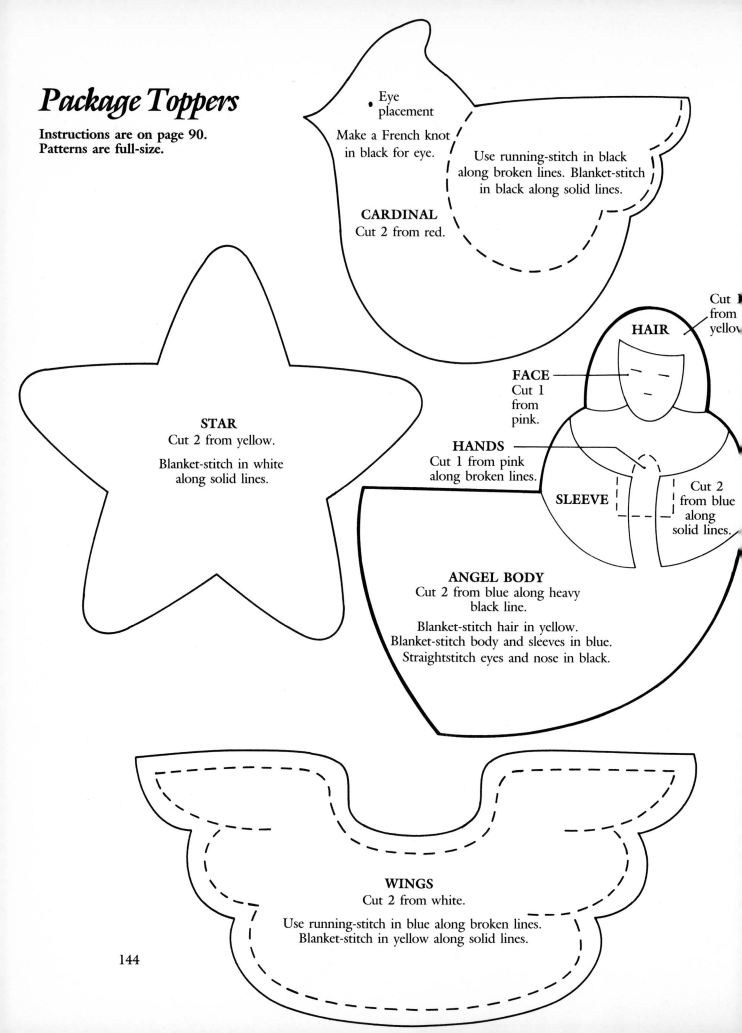

Eye placement

Make a French knot in black for eye.

Use running-stitch in black along broken lines. Blanket-stitch in black along solid lines.

CARDINAL
Cut 2 from red.

HAIR

Cut from yellow

FACE
Cut 1 from pink.

HANDS
Cut 1 from pink along broken lines.

SLEEVE

Cut 2 from blue along solid lines.

STAR
Cut 2 from yellow.

Blanket-stitch in white along solid lines.

ANGEL BODY
Cut 2 from blue along heavy black line.

Blanket-stitch hair in yellow.
Blanket-stitch body and sleeves in blue.
Straightstitch eyes and nose in black.

WINGS
Cut 2 from white.

Use running-stitch in blue along broken lines.
Blanket-stitch in yellow along solid lines.

144

Dress the Table In Festive Color

TABLE RUNNER AND NAPKINS
Instructions are on page 73.
Patterns are full-size and include ¼" seam allowance.

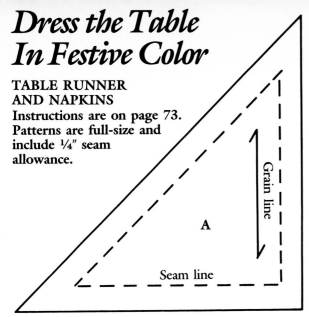

A

Grain line

Seam line

Refer to instructions for number to cut.

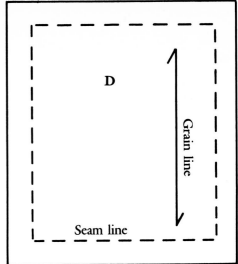

C

Seam line

Grain line

D

Grain line

Seam line

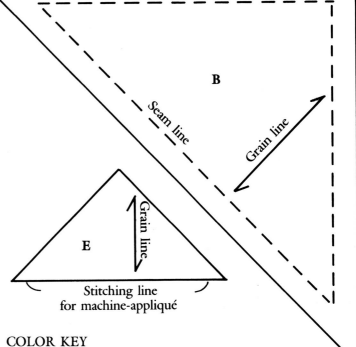

B

Seam line

Grain line

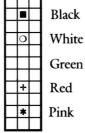

E

Grain line

Stitching line for machine-appliqué

Knit Father Christmas

Instructions are on page 80.

Knitting Chart—Santa

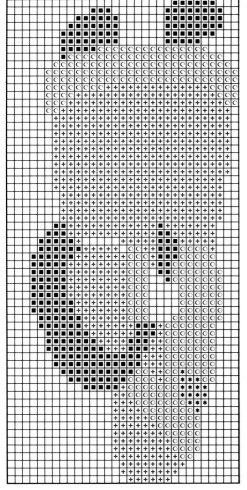

Row 93

Row 31

COLOR KEY

■	Black
O	White
	Green
+	Red
*	Pink

Knitting Chart—Border

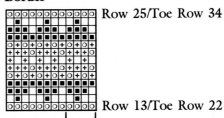

Row 25/Toe Row 34

Row 13/Toe Row 22

Repeat

145

Welcome the Season in Needlepoint

**WHITE CHRISTMAS WELCOME,
STOCKING, AND ORNAMENT**
Instructions are on page 76.
Needlepoint Charts

WELCOME DESIGN

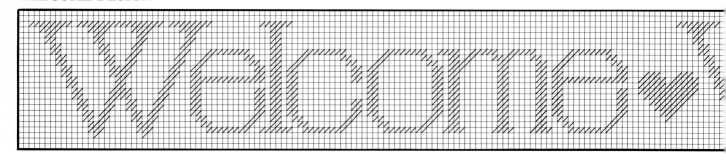

TREE BORDER

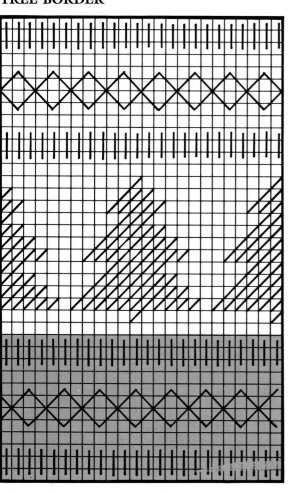

HEART BORDER

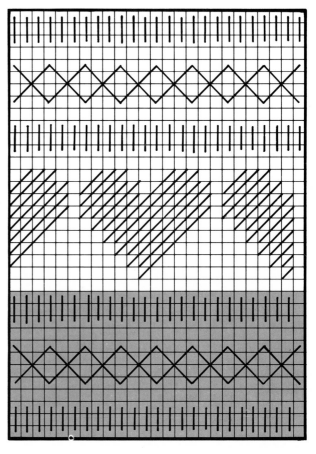

STITCH KEY

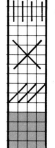

Horiz
Tent

Cross-

Diago
Tent

Omit
Stocki

Stitch designs
all 4 plies of ya

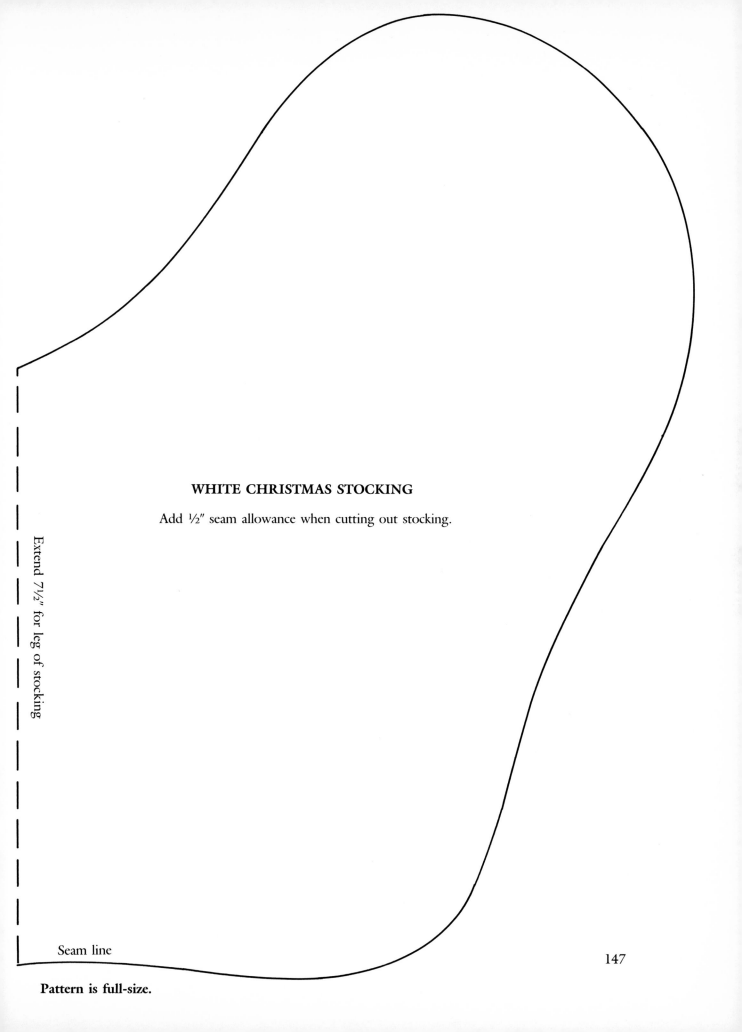

WHITE CHRISTMAS STOCKING

Add ½″ seam allowance when cutting out stocking.

Extend 7½″ for leg of stocking

Seam line

147

Pattern is full-size.

Something For Mom—and Baby, Too

Instructions are on page 96.
Cross-Stitch Chart

Use entire chart for apron bib. Use outlined chart for baby bib. *Do not stitch the outline.*

Center

Center

COLOR KEY
(*Note:* All numbers are for DMC floss.)

Use 2 strands of floss for all cross-stitching. Backstitch using 1 strand of 310 Black. Make French knot berries on wreath using 666 Crimson.

✿	742 Light Orange
⊙	741 Medium Orange
✱	676 Light Saffron
▨	754 Light Salmon
+	605 Medium China Rose

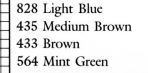

+	956 Dark China Rose
▢	828 Light Blue
•	435 Medium Brown
▶	433 Brown
✕	564 Mint Green

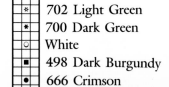

✴	702 Light Green
✱	700 Dark Green
○	White
■	498 Dark Burgundy
•	666 Crimson

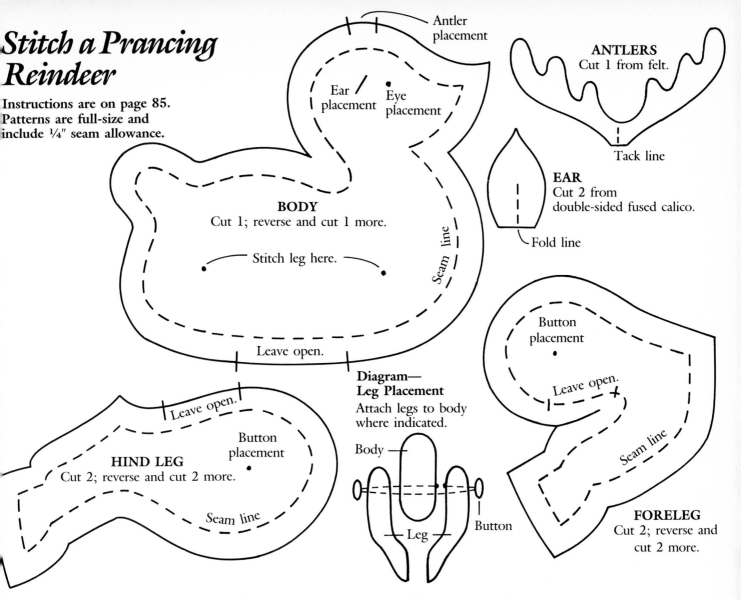

Stitch a Prancing Reindeer

Instructions are on page 85.
Patterns are full-size and
include ¼" seam allowance.

Antler
placement

ANTLERS
Cut 1 from felt.

Ear
placement

Eye
placement

Tack line

BODY
Cut 1; reverse and cut 1 more.

Stitch leg here.

EAR
Cut 2 from
double-sided fused calico.

Seam line

Fold line

Leave open.

Button
placement

**Diagram—
Leg Placement**
Attach legs to body
where indicated.

Leave open.

Leave open.

HIND LEG
Cut 2; reverse and cut 2 more.

Button
placement

Body

Button

Seam line

Seam line

Leg

Button

FORELEG
Cut 2; reverse and
cut 2 more.

Santa Moon Ornament and Wall Hanging

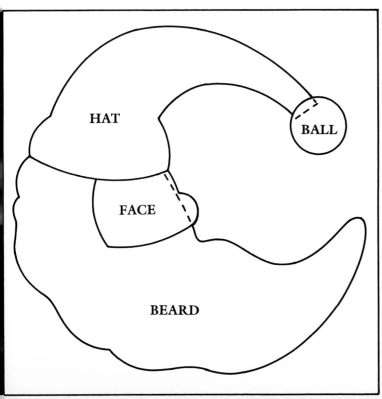

HAT

BALL

FACE

BEARD

Instructions are on page 93.
Patterns are full-size.

Wall Hanging:
Add ¼" seam allowance to patterns.
Cut 2 beards from white, reverse, and
cut 2 more.
Cut 2 faces from pink, reverse, and
cut 2 more.
Cut 2 hats from red, reverse, and cut
2 more.
Cut 4 balls from white.

Ornament:
Cut 1 beard from beige print, reverse,
and cut 1 more.
Cut 1 face from pink, reverse, and
cut 1 more.
Cut 1 hat from red, reverse, and
cut 1 more.
Cut 2 balls from white.

149

Stenciled Cards and Candles

Instructions are on page 70.
Patterns are full-size.

Position stencils on cards
or candles as desired.

Cross-Stitch a Snowman Tote Bag

Instructions are on page 98.
Cross-Stitch Chart

Center

COLOR KEY

○	White
+	317 Gray
■	310 Black
✳	957 Dark Pink
●	321 Red
☆	704 Light Green
◉	699 Medium Green
▼	986 Dark Green
◆	436 Light Brown
▲	433 Medium Brown
✕	809 Sky Blue

(*Note:* All numbers are for DMC floss.)

Use 3 strands for all cross-stitching. Backstitch mouth with 2 strands of 321 Red. Use 2 strands of 310 Black for remaining backstitches.

151

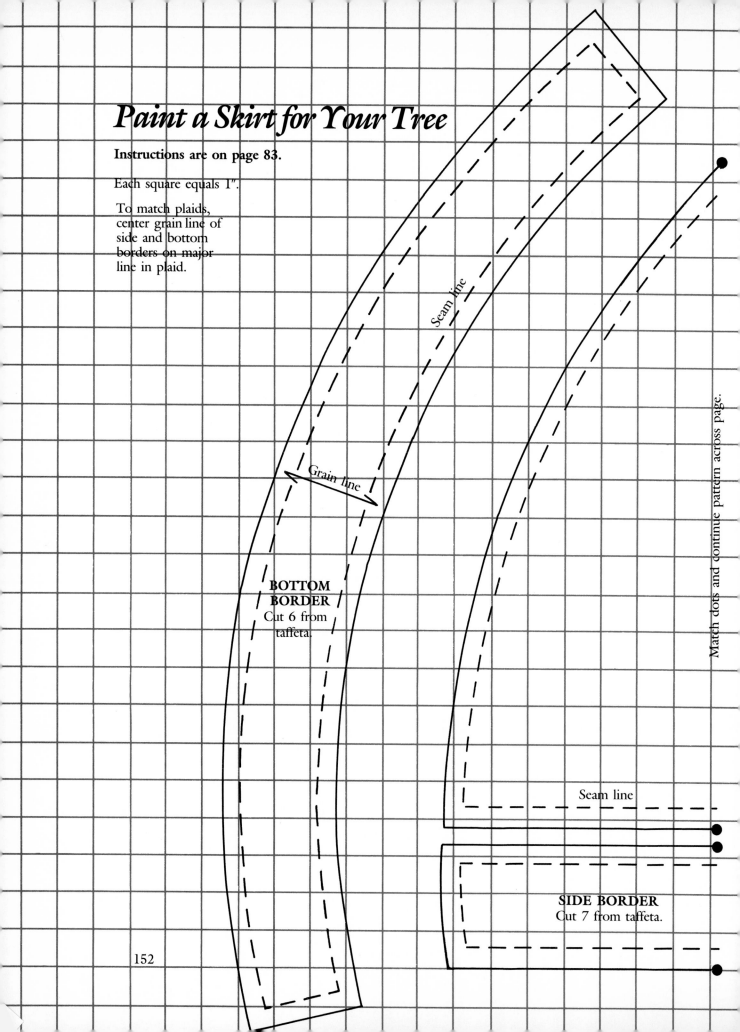

Paint a Skirt for Your Tree

Instructions are on page 83.

Each square equals 1″.

To match plaids, center grain line of side and bottom borders on major line in plaid.

Seam line

Grain line

BOTTOM BORDER
Cut 6 from taffeta.

Seam line

SIDE BORDER
Cut 7 from taffeta.

Match dots and continue pattern across page.

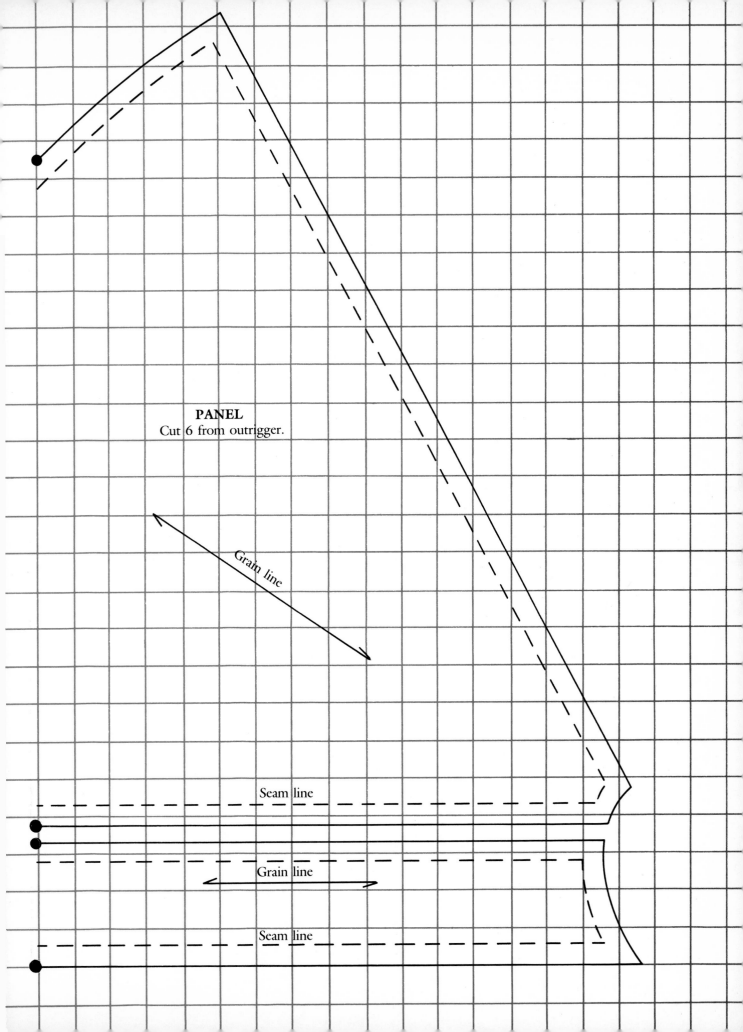

PANEL
Cut 6 from outrigger.

Grain line

Seam line

Grain line

Seam line

A Puzzle for Little Hands

Instructions are on page 91.

Cut along heavy black lines.
Outline puzzle details, using black permanent marker.

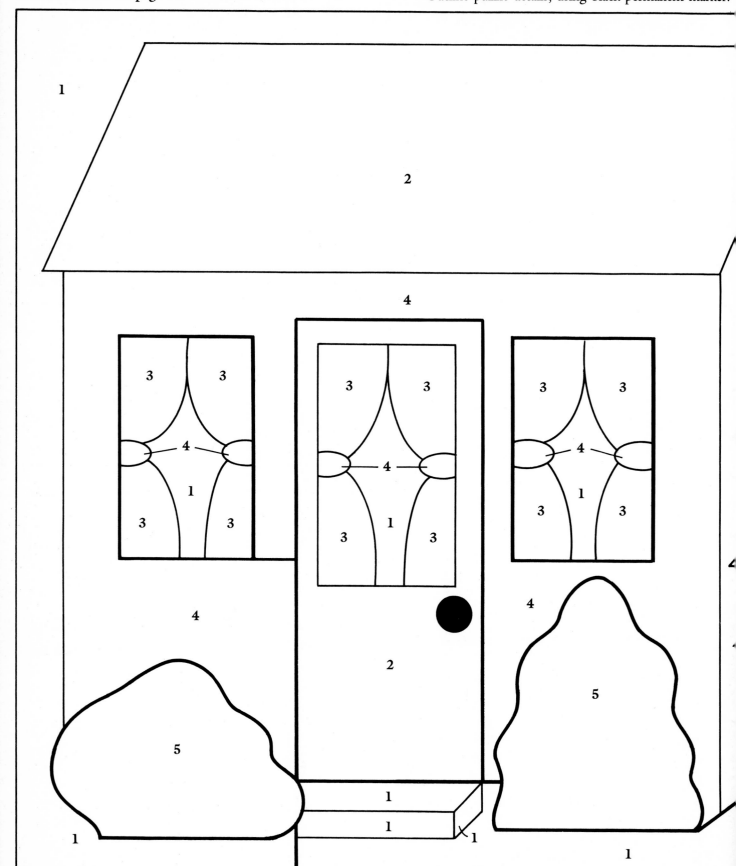

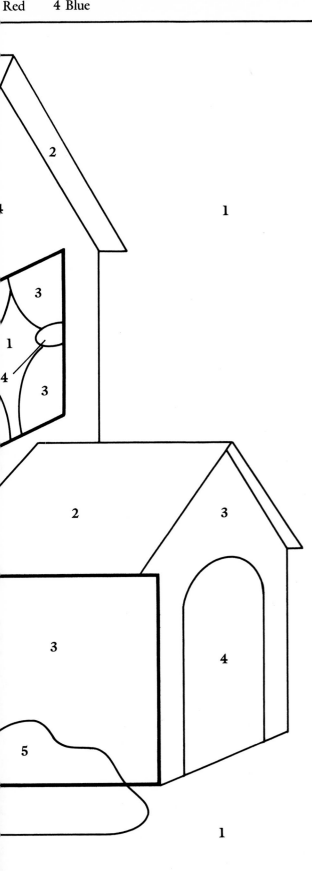

Resources

Write to Ladew Topiary Gardens, 3535 Jarrettsville Pike, Monkton, MD 21111, to obtain additional information about the story featured on pages 4-9.

Additional information about The Wren's Nest (see pages 10-11) can be obtained by writing to The Wren's Nest, 1050 Gordon Street SW, Atlanta, GA 30310.

Learn more about Arlington (see pages 12-13) by writing to Arlington Historical Association, 331 Cotton Avenue SW, Birmingham, AL 35211.

To inquire about Historic Sam Houston Park (see pages 14-17), write to Harris County Heritage Society, 1100 Bagby Street, Houston, TX 77002.

To order cinnamon-dough ornament kits from Willow Oak Flower and Herb Farm (see pages 18-19), write to Maria Price at 8109 Telegraph Road, Severn, MD 21144.

Additional information about Rockwood Museum (see pages 20-24) can be obtained by writing to Rockwood Museum, 610 Shipley Road, Wilmington, DE 19809.

For more information about Rag Bag Loveys (see pages 32-34), write to Carl and Lynn Pendergrass at 4016 Norwood Avenue, Chattanooga, TN 37415.

Write to Martha Elliott-Woodard (see pages 40-43), at 1516 Percheron Court, Chesapeake, VA 23322, to learn more about her work.

For information about stretch lace (Elasti-trim #9) to make balloon balls (see page 71), call Lion Ribbon Co. at 1-800-555-LION.

At Oxmoor House, we are always trying to find ways to serve you better. If you have any requests, craft designs, family recipes or traditions you would like to share, please write to us at *Christmas with Southern Living*, Oxmoor House, P.O. Box 2262, Birmingham, AL 35201.

Contributors

DESIGNERS

Jim Barron, moose, 88.
Lib Bierer, starfish tree, 58.
Curtis Boehringer, needlepoint set, 76.
Jeff Bradley, lantern arrangement, 50; boxwood boas, 60, 61; mantel, 63.
Lena Caron, vegetable wreath, 52.
Carolyn Caswell, rosemary topiary, 59.
Hillary Cheney, potpourri with candle, 66.
Linda Denner, quilted wall hanging, 86.
Susan Z. Douglas, knitted stocking, 80.
Mark Eliason, mantel, 65.
Donna Gallagher, reindeer, 85.
Audrey Griffin, gold tree branch, 59.
Ann Hough, mantel, 64.
June Hudson, fruit in tureen, 54; potpourri with pomegranates, 66.
Linda Rose Johnson, table runner and napkins, 72.
Claude Jones, apple fan, 53.
Heidi T. King, string balls, 71; etched plate, 74.
Evalyn Kirkwood with Imogene Miller, fabric runners, 56.
Jo S. Kittinger, tree skirt, 82; puzzle, 91.
Carol Krob, perforated paper snowflakes, 84.
Nancy Marshall, snowman tote, 98.
Joyce Moore with Imogene Miller, mantel, 62.
Jim Mundy, dog with flowers, 52.
Sandy Ross Norfleet, pineapple badge, 51; natural ornaments, 57.
Elizabeth Nuttle, twin wreaths, 52.
Jody Peterson, cinnamon stick tree, 59.
Janet Rubino, macaroni angel and lamb, 94.
Peg Smith, dining table arrangement, 55.
Eunice Svinicki, crocheted swag, 78.
Louise Switzer, crazy-quilt ornaments, 65.
Norma Swope, hemlock-cone tree, 58.
Carol M. Tipton, Nativity centerpiece, 75; package toppers, 90.
Joan Vibert, Santa wall hanging and ornament, 92.
Lois Winston, apron and bib, 96.

PHOTOGRAPHERS

Van Chaplin, 28, 29, 30, 31, top 56, 62.
Gary Clark, top 13, top 40, 41, 42, 43, 53, bottom 56, bottom 59.
Colleen Duffley, top right 59, 99, 100, 103, 104, 106, 107, 108, 110, 111, 113, 114, 117, 119, 120, 125, 126, 133, 136, 139.
Mary-Gray Hunter, 72, 75, 76, 82, 84, 89, 90, 94, 95.
Hal Lott, 14, 15, 16, 17, 50, 60, 61, 63.
Beth Maynor, 10, 11, 26, 27, 39.
John O'Hagan, cover, title page, contents, 1, 2-3, 4, 5, 6-7, 8, 9, 18, 19, 20, 21, 23, 24, 25, 45, 46, 47, 48, 49, 51, 52, 54, 55, 57, 58, top left 59, 64, bottom 65, 66, 67, 68, 69, 70, 71, 74, 79, 85, 91, 96, 97, 98.
Melissa Springer, 12, bottom 13, 32, 33, 34, 35, 36, 37, 38, 44, top 65, 81, 86, 92, 93.
Gene Woolridge, bottom 40.

PHOTOSTYLISTS

Leslie Byars, 99, 100, 103, 104, 106, 107, 108, 110, 111, 113, 114, 117, 119, 120, 125, 126, 133, 136, 139.
Diane Burnett Lupo, 68.
Joetta Moulden, 14, 15, 16, 17, 50, 60, 61, 63.
Catherine S. Stoddard, cover, title page, contents, 1, 2-3, 25, 45, bottom 65, 67, 69, 70, 71, 74, 75, 76, 79, 82, 84, 89, 90, 91, 94, 95, 98.

Houses on pages 50, 60, 61, and 63 appeared on the Kappa Kappa Gamma Houston Christmas Pilgrimage 1990.

Special thanks to the *Southern Living* Test Kitchens staff for preparing recipes.